Hidden Treasures in Darkness

# Hidden Treasures in Darkness

Jairae Taylor

Meet the World

For permissions, contact:
info@mtwimagesolutions.com

Published by Meet the World Image Solutions
www.mtwimagesolutions.com

Cover design by Meet the World Image Solutions

ISBN: 979-8-9988626-1-8

# Dedication

A matriarch isn't simply a woman who holds the title of head of a family or tribe—she's the soul, the foundation, and the guiding light that shapes the lives of those she touches. My grandmother, Mattie Marie Johnson, was that powerful force for me and countless others. Her legacy was not only built upon the generations she nurtured—children, grandchildren, and great-grandchildren—but also in the profound wisdom she imparted, wisdom that lives on in the written words she left behind.

Grandma Mattie was a poet at heart, a woman with a deep calling to create and share the beauty of her soul through words. She dreamt of publishing a book of poems before she was called home to Glory, and that dream became a reality in *Inspirational Poems*, a work that transcends mere verses. It was an assignment from God, one that ignited a fire within her to capture the journey of the believer with such grace and elegance. Through her poetry, she offered encouragement for anyone walking through a storm, reminding them that even in the darkest days, the light of God's love and faithfulness would guide them through. Her words weren't just ink on paper—they were life-giving, a reminder that with God, all battles are winnable, and all storms can be weathered.

I had the privilege of witnessing firsthand the depth of her faith and the impact of her prayers. Grandma Mattie was the woman who taught me the paramount importance of putting God first. She loved God with an unwavering devotion, and she was a true friend of the Most High. She went before the Lord on many occasions, lifting me in prayer and seeking His protection over my life.

From my earliest days, she saw the dangers that loomed and the attempts of the enemy to lead me astray, and she responded with the full armor of God. She stood in the gap for me, never wavering in her faith or commitment to my well-being.

Her prayers have been answered. As her grandchild, I am a living testament to the power of her faith and intercession. Grandma Mattie, like Abraham, may not have lived to see the fullness of the promises she prayed for, but I am proud to say that her legacy lives on in me and in the lives of those who came after her. No longer are we bound by generational struggles, no longer do we fight just to survive. We are here to thrive, to share the testimonies of God's goodness, and to uplift the body of Christ with the fruit of her labor.

Thank you, Mom-Mom Mattie, for being the unwavering servant of God that you were. Thank you for planting seeds of faith that will continue to bear fruit for generations to come. Your love, your faith, and your prayers will forever live in my heart, guiding me every day of my life.

# Contents

# Acknowledgments

To my mother, Allisa Williams, words can never fully capture the depth of my gratitude for you. From the moment I was conceived, through every heartbeat and breath, you have been there fighting for me, carrying me, and never giving up on me, even during my darkest moments. I know there were times when you felt overwhelmed, when you stayed up countless nights worrying, when my actions caused you pain, and when I tested your patience to the limits. Yet, you always remained steadfast, never letting go, even when the weight of it all seemed too much. You fought battles I will never fully understand, all for the love of me.

Thank you for your unwavering dedication to keeping our family together when the world seemed determined to tear us apart. I'm forever grateful for your strength, for seeking God on my behalf when I didn't have the strength to pray for myself, and for your relentless pursuit of shielding me from the darkness that tried to consume us all. I know there were times when you may have wanted to walk away, but you stayed. You chose to keep your hands on my life, to guide me even when I was resistant, even when I didn't understand your wisdom. You spoke life into me when all I saw was death. You didn't give up, and for that, I will always honor you.

Though I haven't yet walked in the shoes of motherhood, I now see you through a much deeper and more profound lens. I understand, with more clarity than ever, the sacrifices, heartaches, and challenges that come with being a mother. You have shown me what it truly means to love without condition. I commend you, Mom, for never breaking, for never running. Thank you for my life—thank you for being the incredible woman you are.

To my father, David Williams, thank you for showing me, by example, what it truly means to be a father. Your actions have always spoken louder than words, and your quiet strength has been a steady foundation in my life. You have never needed to raise your voice to command respect—your humility, kindness, and consistent presence have done that for you. In every season, your love has been unwavering, your guidance steady, and your heart open.

I didn't always understand the depth of your silence or the meaning behind your gentle ways, but now I see it clearly: in your calm, there was wisdom. In your stillness, there was strength. You have always carried the weight of your family with grace, never asking for praise, always putting others before yourself. You are the kind of man who leads without demanding, loves without condition, and sacrifices without complaint.

You taught me that real strength lies not in dominance, but in self-control. That the mark of a good man is not how loud he roars, but how deeply he listens. You have been a protector, a provider, and a covering in more ways than I can count. And through your life, I have seen the reflection of God's patience, mercy, and quiet endurance.

Thank you for being my anchor, for showing me that integrity doesn't need an audience, and that humility is one of the greatest forms of power. I honor you today and always for being the man who shaped my understanding of love, faith, and what it means to walk in grace.

To my beloved husband, Joshua Taylor, where do I even begin? As a little girl, I used to imagine the kind of man I would one day meet, never knowing you were exactly the man I dreamed of. You are a gift straight from Heaven. Meeting you felt like the beginning of a new chapter, one where my life, which once felt like it was crumbling, was rebuilt in the most beautiful way. You breathed new life into me. With you, I found purpose again, and for the first time in my life, I felt truly seen, loved, and worthy. You have been my rock, my encourager, and my best friend. You helped me rediscover my connection to God, and in doing so, you helped me reconnect with the very essence of who I am. You stood by my side as I shed my old self and embraced the woman I became. Thank you for believing in me, for being my biggest cheerleader, for loving me beyond measure, and for growing with me day by day. You have shown me the true meaning of partnership, love, and faith.

To my mental health team, Lisa Wright and Anthony Trader, thank you for your unwavering support and guidance during my adolescent years. You helped me navigate some of the most challenging moments in my life, and your care has been a beacon of light that guided me through those tumultuous times. I will forever be grateful for the role you played in helping me rebuild my mental and emotional well-being.

To the women who have been instrumental in my spiritual journey—Shelena Cooper, Tiffany Moore, Kimberly King, Tanesia Finney, and Peggy Johnson—your work in God's Kingdom has impacted my life in ways I can't express. You didn't just show me the way back to God; you lovingly guided me through spiritual counseling and prayers, never leaving me behind. You each played a pivotal role in restoring my faith and my purpose, and for that, I will be eternally grateful.

To the body of Christ, I thank you for welcoming me into the house of the Lord with open arms. You have been a spiritual family to me, teaching me the fundamental truths of what it means to live as a believer in Christ. Your love, support, and teachings have helped me uncover the gifts God placed within me. You have provided a space for me to walk in my calling, to serve, and to grow in my faith. In such a short time, you've helped me discover who I am in Christ, shaping my character and my spiritual journey. I am forever grateful for your impact on my life.

To every ministry and individual who has been part of my journey, I pray that the hand of God continues to rest upon you. May His message of salvation echo from your temples and spread to the ends of the earth. May God bless each and every one of you today and forevermore.

Amen.

# Introduction

If you've chosen to give this book a chance, I believe it's no coincidence. I'm certain the Spirit of the Lord has gently drawn you here, and He wants to speak to your heart. Perhaps you find yourself in a dark and lonely place, battling trauma, addiction, abuse, or mental health struggles. Maybe you're weary from running in circles, trapped in a cycle of despair, wondering if you'll ever see the light of day again. You may feel isolated, afraid, and exhausted, unsure of who to turn to for help. Perhaps you feel you've burned bridges with family and friends, or you've cried out to God in your pain but haven't felt His response. You might even be questioning the very existence of God, wondering if belief in Him is just a human construct designed to offer hope in difficult times.

But let me remind you of what God says: "Come to me, all you who are weary and burdened, and I will give you rest." (Matthew 11:28) If you're tired of being broken, feeling as though there's no hope left, I challenge you to believe in His promise of rest. Open your mind and heart and read my testimony. I promise you the darkness you feel is only temporary.

I decree and declare that the Lord, Jehovah-Rapha—the God who heals—meets you right where you are as you read this book. I believe this journey will be one of supernatural healing, where you will experience the love and power of God like never before. As you read, I declare that you will witness signs, miracles, and the manifestation of His Spirit.

In this book, I want to share a few of my personal experiences and encounters that shaped my walk with the Lord. These moments were given to me by the Holy Spirit during my process of transformation. We often believe only education or advice from peers, leaders, or teachers can guide us through life. Yet, the scripture reminds us in John 14:26 (NIV), "But the Advocate, the Holy Spirit, whom the Father will send in my name, will teach you all things and will remind you of everything I have said to you." This verse brings me great comfort because I know I have a loving, all-knowing God who directs my every step.

Though God sends people into my life to share earthly wisdom, He has shown me that He can also provide heavenly wisdom and spiritual truths necessary to navigate this life. He has made it clear to me that following human standards isn't the key to living a fulfilled life. What matters most to God is our obedience to the Holy Spirit. Even when it means setting aside our own ways to follow His, we must trust that He knows what lies ahead on the road we travel each day.

Whenever you feel you are wandering in the wilderness and no one understands your pain, turn to Psalm 77. You'll find that even in biblical times, people faced feelings of isolation and hopelessness, but God responded to those who were close to His heart.

God began to reveal to me the spiritual authority He had placed on my life—an authority that wasn't earned, but given. Just like He gave David the keys to the house of David in Isaiah 22:22: "I will place on his shoulder the key to the house of David; what he opens no one can shut, and what he shuts no one can open"—God also entrusted me with keys. Spiritual keys. These keys weren't just for me; they were for unlocking freedom in others.

This scripture isn't just about doors; it's about authority. David was given divine permission to operate on behalf of God's Kingdom. And in the same way, God has empowered me to speak to the very things that keep people bound, especially in the realm of mental and emotional warfare. I didn't choose this; it was assigned to me. From my own battles and breakthroughs, God gave me a voice to challenge the spirits that torment the minds and hearts of His people.

I've learned the principle of binding and loosing—not just in theory, but in practice. In the name of Jesus, I bind every spirit of suicide, depression, anger, abandonment, fear, and hopelessness. And with the authority of Heaven, I loose the presence of peace, love, joy, clarity, and hope into your life. These are not just nice words; this is spiritual warfare. This is deliverance. This is Kingdom.

May the Spirit of the living God rest upon you as you read this. May chains begin to break, even now. Amen.

In today's world, many are hindered from moving forward because they're trapped in the battle with mental health, believing that a better life is beyond their reach. If you're struggling with these feelings, I want you to know that God sees you, He hears you, and He has the power to transform your life. There is hope for you. Keep reading, keep believing.

# Content Warning

Please be advised that this book contains elements that may not be suitable for some readers. This book was created to raise awareness to adverse experiences that people battle, as well as difficulties people experience when figuring out their relationship with God. Please be aware that drug use, molestation, rape, self-harm, domestic violence, witchcraft, and battles with mental health are present in this book. Readers who may be sensitive to these subjects, please take note. If you are battling with thoughts of suicide, need counseling to heal from trauma, or need help with leaving a domestic violence relationship, please do not hesitate to call the numbers listed below.

**National Hotlines:**

**Crisis Lifeline/Suicide:** call or text 988

**Domestic Violence:** 800-799-7233

**Sexual Assault:** 1-800-656-4673

**Drug Abuse:** 1-800-662-4357

# Activity: Reflecting on Your Heart's Fruit

Take a moment to settle in. Imagine your heart is like a tree. It's deeply rooted within you, shaped by your experiences, your choices, and your beliefs. The branches and fruit growing from this tree represent the parts of you that others see—the way you behave, interact, and show up in the world.

Now, close your eyes for a second and think about the things in your life that have caused you pain, frustration, or turmoil. These are often the seeds of bad fruit—the acts of the flesh we hear about in Galatians 5:19–21: sexual immorality, impurity, idolatry, hatred, jealousy, selfishness, anger, envy, drunkenness, and many more.

Perhaps, like me, you can relate to some of these behaviors. I'll be honest: for a long time, I didn't even realize I was bearing this kind of fruit. I was so caught up in what I thought was normal, unaware of the internal damage I was causing myself and the people around me. But the reality was, my heart had become like a tree that bore spoiled, rotten fruit.

This fruit didn't just affect me; it affected everyone who came near me. My words and actions were like poison, slowly spreading, causing mental, emotional, and even physical harm to those I loved. I didn't see it at the time, but the truth was, I was unknowingly hurting myself and others. And it nearly cost me everything.

Now, I want you to reflect on your own heart for a moment. If any of the actions or attitudes listed in Galatians 5 resonate with you, it's okay. It's okay because you're not alone. I want to tell you there's hope. No matter how deep your roots of negativity or destructive behavior might be, God's love is greater. He sees the brokenness and struggle, and He wants to help you heal.

You may be thinking, "But where do I begin?" Here's the first step: acknowledge what's not right. Acknowledge the things about yourself you wish were different. You see, God revealed to me that the key to transformation was honesty to face my flaws and allow Him to work in me. He doesn't expect perfection; He simply asks for your openness, your willingness to let Him help you grow into who He created you to be.

Now, I want you to picture that tree again as your heart. On the next page, you'll see a drawing of this tree. I want you to take a moment to reflect on what's growing on your branches. What kind of fruit are you bearing right now? Is it fruit of anger, bitterness, jealousy, or fear? Or is it fruit that nourishes, uplifts, and heals?

Take a deep breath, and as you look at the tree, start by listing the things you're struggling with—the fruit you're not proud of. Write down the areas where you feel there's work to be done. These might be emotional struggles, negative patterns in your life, or toxic behaviors that you've learned over time.

It's important that you take this step of reflection. I encourage you to write with vulnerability and honesty because in doing so, you are starting the process of healing. It's like uncovering the root cause of those bad fruits so God can gently remove them and replace them with something good that reflects His Spirit.

When you do this, you allow space for God to work within you. You allow Him to plant new seeds in the soil of your heart, seeds of love, joy, peace, kindness, patience, goodness, faithfulness, gentleness, and self-control. (Galatians 5:22) These are the fruits that reflect God's nature and will transform your life from the inside out.

Once you've reflected on the fruit that needs to go, let's take this next step together. I want you to consider four things you can begin doing to nourish your heart and grow new, good fruit. These actions don't have to be monumental. They can be small, intentional steps toward becoming the person you're meant to be—someone who embodies God's love and grace.

Perhaps you could commit to practicing kindness, letting go of anger, seeking peace in difficult situations, or learning to forgive. Whatever it is, take time to write down your thoughts. Your heart is the soil, and the good fruit will come as you nourish it with intentionality and love.

On the next page, you will find space to write down those four things. Think of them as the tools God will use to help you grow a new tree that bears the fruit of His Spirit. Each time you practice these actions, you'll take steps toward healing and transformation. You'll be nourishing your heart, allowing it to become a vessel of goodness and love. I encourage you to keep this page close and revisit it often. Remember transformation takes time, but with God's help, the fruit of the Spirit will grow abundantly within you.

Refer to the following scripture as
an overall example of this activity:
LUKE 6:43–45
and GALATIANS 5:19–23

Fruit to improve on      Fruit, i,e. strengths

## Disclaimer

This exercise shouldn't take the place of any doctor's orders. Please seek medical advice and God in your matters for Him to lead you on what to do. This book provides several resources to receive help and that's OKAY! God has created resources in our communities to help us grow, so seek the appropriate resources for a beautiful solution.

## Nourishing Your Soul

# There Is No Light in the Dark

From a young age, God placed His hand on my life. I didn't fully understand it then, but even in my childhood, I could sense I was set apart for something greater. I wasn't just going through life; I was being prepared. God appointed me early, calling me into service before I truly knew what that meant. And because of that calling, the enemy came after me hard. The attacks didn't wait until I was older or more prepared. They came in my youth, when I was most vulnerable, trying to break me before I could ever step into my purpose. The enemy saw the anointing on my life even when I couldn't, and he did everything in his power to silence the calling before it could speak.

If I could speak honestly, the first thing I'd admit is I didn't fully believe in God at the beginning. Growing up, church was a family tradition passed down through generations of pastors, ministers, bishops, and musicians. It was just something we did, no questions asked. Sunday mornings were routine, the songs were familiar, and the sermons felt like background noise. I was surrounded by the structure of religion, but the relationship with God hadn't yet been made real to me. It was in my blood, but not yet in my heart.

But even then, God was speaking. Even when I didn't understand Him, He understood me. When I didn't believe in Him, He believed in the purpose He placed inside me. My journey didn't start with a burning bush moment; it started with a silent whisper in the dark. It started with restlessness in my spirit, questions that couldn't be answered, and a deep yearning to find meaning beyond the routine. That's the thing about God's call: it often finds you before you even know what you're looking for.

These days, I hear so many people say, "I'm chosen," or "I'm prophetic," as if it's a badge of honor to wear lightly. But what they often don't realize is that with being chosen comes pain. With anointing comes fire. Being called by God is not glamorous. It's costly. I've witnessed countless people who are eager for the title, hungry for the authority, but completely unaware of the weight that comes with it. They want the oil, but not the crushing, the elevation, but not the isolation.

But the process is necessary. The fire refines. The suffering molds. The rejection strengthens. The turmoil prepares. Every storm, every heartbreak, every moment of silence when it felt like God had forgotten me were all part of the training ground. You can't carry the glory of God without first carrying the weight of His process.

Many are called, yes, but only those who endure the process can walk in true power. Because the journey to fulfilling God's calling is never easy; it's a road marked by spiritual warfare, deep valleys, and moments of brokenness. But it's in those places that God shapes warriors. And when the time comes, those same battles that once tried to destroy you become the very testimony that confirms your authority. As you read this book you will see some of the hardest battles I endured throughout my life that was trying to destroy me from conception to present moments. I share these moments not for a person to pity my journey, but to be a living testimony of how God will keep his hands upon you even in the darkest moments of your life and how he will always lead you back to him if you are willing to seek him for true understanding.

I can recall early on in my childhood, I found myself questioning everything. *Why did people say God was good when bad things happened to good people? Why pray to a God who seemed silent and invisible?*

No one could give me a satisfying answer. In my family, questioning faith was disrespectful so I kept my doubts to myself, holding onto them year after year.

Over time, the lack of answers made me doubt who God was to me. I had never been taught how to build a personal relationship with God through demonstration. Most of the time I was told to talk to God the way I would talk to anyone, but I didn't understand how to truly connect with Him or what it meant to sit in His presence. I didn't know how to hear from Him, and when I did, I had no idea what to do with it. I gave up trying to understand, relying on my elders to pray for me, thinking I had to approach God in the "right" way for my prayers to be heard.

I would listen to my grandmother and her children pray, their words flowing effortlessly, and I felt a deep sense of awe. Their prayers were powerful, and I thought that was how I was supposed to pray—perfectly, without hesitation. But being a perfectionist, I found myself intimidated. I couldn't find the right words or organize the chaotic thoughts in my mind, so I didn't seek God at all unless I was in trouble. And every time I cried out to Him, He saved me— only for me to end up in even worse situations. It was a cycle I didn't know how to break, and it's a struggle many face today. God delivers us, but if we return to the same sin, what's the point?

True repentance, I realized, isn't just asking for forgiveness; it's turning away from what caused us to stumble. At the time, I used God as my escape, calling on Him when

I was overwhelmed by my own choices. I sought after my own desires and ignored what my spirit longed for—a peaceful, real relationship with God.

When I wasn't desperate, I let my flesh lead me into shameful actions, thinking if I stayed out of His sight, He wouldn't see my mistakes. But the flesh and the spirit are always in conflict. I wanted to follow my own desires, which led to disobedience. God, I learned, just wants us to listen to Him. He gives wisdom and direction, but many people, myself included, have spent years chasing approval through man-made rules, believing that strict performance somehow equates to righteousness. But true obedience isn't about religion; it's about relationship. It's about learning to trust His voice above all others.

For me, that lesson didn't just begin in adulthood; it dates all the way back to the womb. Long before I could speak or choose for myself, my life was already a testimony of obedience. The enemy tried to orchestrate a plan to make my parents go against what God had destined. Fear was planted through the voices of medical professionals, telling them I would be born with Down syndrome and urging them to terminate the pregnancy.

It was through my mother's obedience—her willingness to trust the still, small voice of God over the loud and logical opinions of man—that she chose to carry me anyway. She followed God's leading, even when it didn't make sense. Though there were complications, I was born healthy. She delivered me in just thirty-two minutes without a doctor present.

I entered the world still enclosed in the amniotic sac, and a nurse rushed in just in time to tear it open and save me. That moment should have been miracle enough, but it was only the beginning.

My mother soon realized the true battle wouldn't be my birth—it would be the process of raising me. I was diagnosed with chronic asthma, and my childhood was filled with hospital visits. One time, during an asthma attack, my mother rushed me to the hospital. The doctors inserted an IV wrong, and they feared I would lose my arm. But God—He healed me, and I still have all my limbs.

On another occasion, as I struggled to breathe, my mother stayed calm and coached me through the fear. I would later learn that each breath we take—each inhale and exhale—can be a prayer, breathing the name of God. Through all those years of fighting for breath, God was with me, sustaining me.

Despite all the challenges, my parents kept pushing through. Raising five children with their own needs was no easy task. I can only imagine how exhausted they were, but they kept going, doing the best they could.

When I was just a few months old, my mother took me to her church, where a prophet declared over me that I was anointed, and God would use me mightily for His Kingdom. That word was spoken before my first birthday, but it took over twenty years for me to fully accept my calling and understand God's purpose for me.

By the time I was a teenager, I had lost almost all hope that the God my family spoke of would ever save me. I was deep in a pit, and I didn't think I would ever see the light again. I couldn't fathom how a God so good would allow someone like me to be stuck in a pit so deep and filthy, one I thought I'd never escape. Every day felt like I was sinking lower, my soul growing heavier with each passing moment. The darkness seemed to consume me more completely as I unwittingly agreed to the lies the enemy whispered in my ear—death threats I had been exposed to since the moment I was conceived.

I remember retreating to my room, locking the door, and losing myself in a storm of emotions. I would spend hours upon hours—sometimes fourteen or more—crying until I fell asleep from sheer exhaustion. It wasn't the tears that pained me the most, though. It was the relentless mental torment I couldn't understand or escape.

The enemy had planted seeds in my head that made no sense, but somehow felt like truths. And though I could never find the words to speak of it, I feared the very thought of giving voice to what had already taken root inside me. I felt utterly trapped, as though my soul was being suffocated with no way out.

There was a time in my life when my silence screamed louder than my voice. I wrote suicide letters and wrapped ropes around my neck in hopes of building confidence enough to fully go through with killing myself. I couldn't articulate the storm inside me. My emotions were buried beneath trauma, confusion, and a rage I didn't know how to name. My mind had become a battlefield, and I was losing. The devil didn't need to shout; he just whispered, and in that vulnerable moment, I listened.

One number echoed in my thoughts like a drumbeat I couldn't silence. Six. I grabbed a pen like it was instinct—maybe even invitation—and began to write 6 … 6 … 6 over and over. Relentless. Possessed. It wasn't just ink. It was intention. Something in me was trying to break free or break down. And in my pain, I didn't realize I was giving hell permission.

That number wasn't just random; it was a message. A mockery of everything I had been taught to believe. In Christian understanding, 666 represents the mark of the beast, the antichrist, opposition to everything holy. And yet, there I was, writing it willingly, not because I was evil, but because I was empty.

I grew up in a house full of prayer and praise, raised by warriors who knew how to touch Heaven. But pain has a way of making you forget what you were taught. That day, I let darkness in. I wasn't just attacked—I agreed. I made a silent covenant with everything I was born to fight against.

I locked myself in my room, hoping isolation would give me clarity. Instead, it became a tomb. I sat on the floor, heart pounding, desperate to release everything trapped inside, but no words came. Just numbers. So, I kept writing 6 ... 6 ... 6, and then my body gave out. A violent tremor shook me to my core. I dropped the pen. My head hit the floor. The world spun. My vision blurred. I felt myself separating, drifting. Watching from above as my body lay motionless. I heard voices—my parents, my sister's husband—but I couldn't respond. I was there, but not really. I had crossed a line, and I knew it. It was the closest I had ever come to giving up completely.

But God. Even in my rebellion, He was fighting for me. Even in my silence, He heard me. The same God I had ignored had sent people to find me. Rescue me. Remind me that I still belonged to Him.

I completely lost my memory that night. The doctors had no answers. No medical explanation. No logic to grasp onto—just a weak suggestion that maybe I'd had a seizure. But that didn't explain the terror in my family's eyes as they gathered around my hospital bed whispering desperate prayers over me.

Hours later, as suddenly as it had vanished, my memory returned. Just like that, I was discharged and sent back into the world as if nothing had happened. But something *had* happened. Something they couldn't see.

My parents dragged me from one therapist to the next, hoping someone could reach me. But I had built a fortress

around myself, a wall so high and impenetrable that no pro-
fessional could break through. They tried. They all tried.
But I sat in those therapy rooms silent and distant, refusing
to let them in.

The only solution the psychiatrists could offer was a
prescription. Antidepressants, they said. A chemical imbal-
ance, they called it. Low serotonin, the hormone that con-
trols mood, memory, stress, addiction, and sleep.

Science had an explanation for my suffering, but no
cure. My pain wasn't just chemical; it was deeper than that.
It was spiritual. That was something no doctor, no therapist,
or no pill could fix. My family prayed and took me to Christian counselors, believing faith could reach me where medicine had failed. But nothing worked. Nothing. And then,
just days before my fourteenth birthday, they sent me away.
A mental facility. A place for the broken. I was gone.

I had planned my death during my freshman year.
Afraid my family would find my body, I took a full bottle of
Tylenol into the bathroom stall at school and took a handful
of pills. I barely registered the knocking on the stall door before it swung open. My best friend stood there, eyes wide
with horror. In that instant, my fate was sealed.

Everything blurred after that. Police. Handcuffs. The
walk of shame. Hospital lights. Voices speaking over me as
if I weren't even there.

I was under surveillance for seventy-two hours, forced
to drink thick, black charcoal that tasted like dirt and regret.
It was sheer disgust going down, and soon, I was retching
into a bucket, my body purging itself from both ends. The
humiliation was unbearable. I wasn't just sick; I was exposed. Vulnerable. Trapped in a cycle of shame while my
grandmother and parents stood by my hospital bed, praying
through their tears. Their hands trembled as they clutched
mine, begging God to save me.

Once my system was clear, they strapped me onto a stretcher and loaded me into an ambulance. I stared at the ceiling, my mind numb. This was real. This was happening.

The facility was nothing like I imagined, yet somehow, exactly like what I'd seen on TV. A padded room. A strait-jacket. Clothes stripped away and replaced with a flimsy, degrading "crazy suit." They kept me under surveillance again, their eyes on me at all times, as if I were a danger to myself and everyone around me.

The room was small. Cold. More of a jail cell than a place of healing. If I needed the bathroom, I had to call for a guard. Privacy was a luxury I no longer had.

One night, we went on lockdown after a fight broke out in another block. I sat there, staring at the walls, listening to the distant sound of screaming. And then, I looked at the other kids around me. Their eyes were hollow. Empty. As if life had already abandoned them. They were children, just like me, but their faces carried the weight of eternal death. I was troubled. I knew that. But I didn't belong there. Not like this.

The first time my parents visited, my mother brought me a pair of Mickey Mouse pajamas that said "Smile" across the front. Before she left, she squeezed my hand and told me to remember the lyrics to Kirk Franklin's song "Smile." At the time, I hated that song. I wish I had given these lyrics a chance to truly speak to my soul while I was locked in that mental facility.

At the time, I was so overwhelmed by pain, confusion, and hopelessness that I almost gave up completely. My mind was clouded, my heart was heavy, and it felt like no one—not even God—could reach me in that place. But now, looking back, I realize that if I had truly taken in the words in that moment—if I had let them sink into the deepest parts of my brokenness—they could have given me a spark of hope. Those lyrics were more than just a song; they were a lifeline.

If I had clung to that truth, I might have seen that even in the isolation and darkness, Heaven was still reaching for me. That God hadn't forgotten me. That joy, healing, and light were still possible even there.

I was released a few days later, but it surely didn't mean I was released mentally from bondage. Nothing could save me from the devil. By the time I turned sixteen, I had been through several traumatic experiences that should have taken me out. Molestation was the root of it all. The spirit of perversion is a harmful force that distorts what is pure and good, especially in our thoughts, feelings, and actions. It twists healthy and natural expressions of love and intimacy into something damaging and wrong. It changes the way we see relationships, sex, and personal boundaries, turning them into things of control and exploitation. Ephesians 5:3 reminds us that God's design for relationships is pure and holy, and anything that strays from that is harmful to our well-being. Molestation is a painful result of this spirit of perversion. It's an abuse of trust, a violation of innocence, and a misuse of power.

I was never the same after being molested. My boundaries were broken, and I was forced into a distorted idea of what intimacy looked like. I was not only physically scarred, but the emotional damage was significant. This caused me to have trust issues throughout life and twisted how I perceived myself. I felt empty and had no sense of self worth. It controlled me from as far back as my memories allowed me to go. I turned to porn, but that was never enough. I would feel my body pulsate and had no idea what it meant except to release my sexual desires.

Perversion at its core is a lie, a counterfeit of the pure love, trust, and respect I should have encountered throughout my earlier years of life. Instead, I continued chasing perversion because it was all I knew.

I gave away my virginity to Tre, a boy I met in Bible school because being wanted by someone of my choice made me head over heels, never realizing I had no idea what true love meant or even felt like. I felt emotionally numb, like I was drifting through each day, disconnected from myself, my body, and my emotions. The weight of my past trauma made it very hard to truly feel anything, leaving me in a state of constant dissociation. When we kissed, when our bodies touched and our hands explored, something shifted.

One evening, my parents confronted me about having sex and I admitted to it nonchalantly. My mother took my phone and threatened to ground me so I would have no way to communicate with him. My sister provoked the situation. My mother stood over me like she was going to hit me, so I stood up to defend myself. I became so angry I no longer cared if she was my mother and even considered getting in position to fight her. However, before I could finish my thoughts, my father jumped between us to de-escalate the situation.

I went back to my room and fell deeper into a hole. I never wanted to hurt my mother in that moment. It was just that, in my pain, I thought I had found something—someone—who could help me navigate the storm inside me. My hypersexuality felt like a relentless force I couldn't escape, and in him, I convinced myself I had found a way to cope, to fill the emptiness I couldn't articulate.

When my mother forbade me to speak to him, it wasn't just a simple loss of a young love situation. It felt like the last thread that held me together was being ripped away. He was the one person who, in the chaos of my brokenness, made me feel like our twisted connection could somehow be a fix to my internal battles. Losing him in that moment felt like losing the only thing that made the overwhelming pain of my existence bearable, even if it was just for a little while. The thought of losing him was gut wrenching. The one guy I felt comfortable to be myself with and get my needs met was now being blocked by my parents. I found my phone one day and contacted Tre to let him know what happened. It didn't take long for my mother to catch me communicating with him, and she gave me a whooping I would never forget.

From that moment on, I no longer had contact with him. I began seeking love in all the wrong places from both male and female. I would have sex with guys and flirt with girls to satisfy the cravings. Being hypersexual became my way of trying to fill a void. Each encounter, each fleeting moment of connection, felt like the only way to escape the emptiness inside me, but afterward, I was left with an even deeper sense of hollowness. It was as if I had been chasing something I could never truly grasp, like being led down the yellow brick road full of hope and desire, only to reach a dead end. The disappointment hit hard, leaving me feeling lost, like I had poured myself into something that promised fulfillment but only gave me more pain in return.

I desperately sought comfort in those moments, but each time, I only felt more alone and more broken. I didn't want to feel those feelings, so I began to experiment with drugs. Anything to numb the pain and allow me to escape from the hell on earth was worth trying. I began to take my father's OxyCodone around the age of fifteen. I would take pills before I got on the bus for school and would be high throughout the day. It made me feel free from the sexual urges of wanting to be wanted. It made me not care about anyone or anything.

I remember my parents confronting me about taking my father's pills, but I denied it. They locked up the medicine and hid the key. I was able to find the keys on some days and get high, but on days I wasn't high, I felt sick from the withdrawals. I began hanging with some guys at school who told me about over-the-counter medications that would give me the same effect. I would skip school with them to get high, considering myself to be one of the fellas. I never considered what could happen to me.

One day, a guy named Q invited me upstairs to a bedroom. He closed the door and locked it. I honestly didn't think anything of it until he laid on top of me and I pushed him away. He tried to talk me out of saying no, but I continued to plead with him. He rubbed on my body and I begged him to stop. Once he noticed I was crying, he backed away from me and I left the house ashamed. I never looked at him the same after that. Every time he saw me, he would apologize, telling me he thought I wanted it.

If I'm being honest, I was very flirty in school, constantly laughing, smiling, or making eye contact with someone. It wasn't because I wanted to be with someone or because I craved romance. No, it was deeper than that. It was about being seen, about feeling like I mattered for once. I wanted to feel noticed, like my presence held weight, like someone, anyone, would take a second look past the walls I had built and truly see that I was under pressure, trapped in a dark place!

It was like performing on stage, each playful wink or smirk a desperate plea for attention, a silent cry to be acknowledged in a world that felt so large and isolating. Every flirtatious word, every glance, was a tiny moment where I could feel alive, even if it was just for a second.

Luckily, two high school teachers took me under their wings. Dr. Bowen and Ms. McDonald kept me behind after class to speak life into me. I wondered what they saw in me. One of them said my eyes held so much history and destiny within them. I never understood what that meant, so I tucked it away in the back of my mind and continued to seek the thrills that awaited me in the dark: over-the-counter drugs, opioids, edibles, and constantly having sex until I crashed. I was still empty, lonely, and misunderstood, no matter how much I chased those temporary moments of fulfillment.

One day, the urge for pills vanished. The thought of it made me sick to my stomach, so I stopped instantly. Looking back on it, I now believe God took the habit away from me before I was too far gone. At that age, I had no idea that quitting pills all at once could send my body into complete chaos. The shaking started first—just a little tremor in my hands—but soon, waves of nausea hit me so hard I could barely stand. My skin felt tight, my heart pounded like it was trying to break free from my chest, and a deep, unbearable cold settled into my bones, no matter how many blankets I wrapped around myself. This was followed by sweats that made my body feel like I was burning in hell.

I didn't understand what was happening. I thought maybe I was dying. But even as my body betrayed me, I kept it all to myself. I curled up in the dark, too scared to ask for help, too ashamed to admit I had let myself get to this point. No one knew about the battle I fought alone in that room—the long nights, the nightmares, the way my mind twisted against me. And when it finally ended, when I could finally breathe without feeling like I was drowning, I still didn't tell a soul because who would want to be exposed as a teenaged junkie?

Shortly after my body started rejecting the pills, something inside me snapped. I gave up one thing just to indulge in something far more sinister. I didn't just lose control; I gave it away, recklessly throwing myself into situations where I knew I could be hurt, where I knew someone could take advantage of me. And I didn't care.

I welcomed the danger. I sought it out. Every bad decision, every risky place I wandered into, was all a silent dare, a test to see if fate would finally take me out because I couldn't do it myself. I didn't have the courage to end my own life, but if someone else did it for me? If my blood ended up on someone else's hands? That felt easier. That felt like an escape.

I should have known better, but I still decided to go with the flow of life. That thought gnawed at me as I sat on my "friend's" couch, pretending I belonged there. I had so few real friends that I latched onto whatever connection I could find, even when it felt forced. To be honest, maybe she never truly saw me as a friend. After all, I had once been with her baby daddy before we met. But I was too naïve, too desperate for someone to make me feel like I mattered. I ignored the tension, ignored the way she side-eyed me when she thought I wasn't looking, and ignored the unspoken history between us, and I convinced myself this was friendship.

That afternoon felt normal until her cousin showed up. He had just gotten out of jail, his presence thick and heavy in the small space. He barely acknowledged me at first, but the air shifted the moment he walked in. Maybe I should have left then. Maybe I should have listened to the small voice inside me that told me something wasn't right.

But I didn't listen. I never did.

The night stretched on, and I stayed. My friend shared a bed with her child, so I told her I'd be fine on the couch. I didn't ask questions when her cousin stayed, too. Maybe I should have.

He sat next to me, close enough that I could feel the heat of his body. He handed me an alcoholic drink, and I took it. It burned my throat, numbed my thoughts, and dulled the ache in my chest that never seemed to go away. I welcomed it. I wanted to disappear into that hazy nothingness, wanted to escape myself, because deep down, I already knew how this night would end.

I had walked into this moment like I had walked into so many others—reckless, uncaring, daring the world to do its worst. I had told myself over and over again: If I die, let it be at someone else's hands. If I bleed, let it not be by my own doing.

And then this grown man fresh out of jail was on top of me. The world went silent. My mind shut down. My body became something distant, something separate from me. I floated away, slipping into that familiar, detached space where nothing could reach me—not the weight of him nor the sound of my own heartbeat hammering in my ears. I wanted to fight, but my limbs wouldn't allow me to move. I wanted to scream, but the thought of "this is what you wanted" flooded my thoughts, so I let it happen.

When it was over, I didn't cry. I didn't scream. I just laid there, staring at the ceiling, my insides hollowed out, my soul slipping through the cracks of my skin.

The next morning, as I stepped outside, the weight of what happened settled over me like a thick fog. The guilt gnawed at my bones, whispering cruel truths in my ears:

*You had no business being there.*

*You let this happen.*

*This is what you wanted, right?*

That moment haunted me, but as time moved on and I crossed the threshold from seventeen to eighteen, something in me hardened. I told myself I was grown now, that being legal meant being in control. I was done letting people tell me what to do or how to live. By the time I reached my freshman year of college, I thought I had life figured out. I made my own choices. I wrote my own rules. I believed no one could take anything from me unless I allowed it. What I didn't realize then was that pain doesn't respect age, and trauma doesn't wait for permission.

So, when I reconnected with Tia, an old friend from elementary school, and she invited me to her campus homecoming party, I didn't hesitate. The idea of stepping into a real college party for the first time thrilled me. It felt like the beginning of something new, something exciting.

But my mom didn't see it that way.

"Please, don't go," she begged me that night, her voice tight with fear. "I have a bad feeling."

I rolled my eyes, brushing off her warning. She was always worrying, always seeing danger where there was none. I told her I was grown now, that I could handle myself. I told her to stop treating me like a child.

Still, as she drove me to the campus, the air inside the car felt heavy, thick with something unspoken. She kept glancing at me like she wanted to say more, like she wanted to turn the car around. And when we finally pulled up, she grabbed my hand.

"I love you," she whispered. "Please be safe."

Something about the way she said it made me hesitate for just a second. She never said things like that. But I was too excited, too eager to finally taste "real" freedom, so I smiled, promised her I'd be fine, and got out of the car.

I never should have.

Tia's dorm was small and cluttered, but it felt alive with the kind of energy I had been craving. Another girl, Bree, came over, and we started drinking half a pint of peach Paul Mason, the cheap burn of it making me laugh. It was nothing I wasn't used to. Just drinks and fun as we passed the bottle around. When Bree left, Tia and I headed to the main campus.

"Here," she said, when we arrived, handing me a cup. "My friend makes the best drinks."

I glanced down at the cup in my hand, filled with a green liquid. She told me it was a mixed drink, so I didn't think twice. Why would I? This was a party. This was what people did. So I took the cup and swallowed it in a few quick gulps, expecting the usual warmth in my chest and that familiar, carefree buzz to follow.

But this wasn't like any other drink I'd had before. At first, everything felt normal. The bass thumped through the air, wrapping around me, pulling me into the music. I started dancing, my body moving freely, lost in the moment. A group of guys followed us around, trying to dance with us. I laughed and brushed them off, thinking nothing of it.

Then, suddenly, the room tilted. It was subtle at first, the way the walls seemed to shift, the way the lights flickered just a little too much. My vision blurred at the edges, as if I were looking through a foggy window. The laughter around me became distant, muffled, like it was coming from underwater. I tried to focus and shake it off, but my body wasn't listening. My legs felt heavy, like they were no longer mine. My arms tingled, and my fingers felt numb. I didn't think I was *that* drunk. Panic crept in, cold and sharp. Something wasn't right.

I spotted a security guard near the door and, in a haze, I stumbled toward him. I tried to make it look playful, like I was just dancing my way over, trying to get his attention without raising alarm. My lips struggled to form words as I fought to ask for help. But just as I was about to reach him, Tia appeared out of nowhere, yanking me back with a tight grip on my arm.

"No, come on," she said sharply. "Let's go."

I tripped, my knees giving out. The floor rose up to meet me, and I hit the ground hard. I couldn't get up. Everything was spinning. The room stretched and warped, and faces twisted into shadows. My breath became shallow gasps. My body wouldn't move the way I wanted it to. I tried to speak, but the words tangled on my tongue. I wasn't drunk. I was drugged!

Tia guided me out of the building. The night air hit my skin like a slap, but it did nothing to clear my mind. I fumbled for my phone, my fingers clumsy and useless. Somehow, I managed to call the only person I could think of: Tre, the boy who had taken my virginity.

"Tre ... " I said, my voice barely a whisper. "Come get me."

"Where are you?" he asked, but the words didn't make sense in my head. I didn't know how to answer. I didn't know where I was. My mind was slipping away, spiraling into darkness. He hung up and I stared at my phone, my vision doubling. I didn't know how to call him back.

I heard footsteps behind us. Tia and I weren't alone. A group of men trailed behind us, their voices low, their eyes locked on me. My heart pounded a deep, sickening thud against my ribs. I could feel them closing in, feel their presence like a shadow crawling over my skin. This was it. This was the moment I had been waiting for, wasn't it? The moment I had told myself would be easier than doing it myself. *If I die, let it be at someone else's hands.* I had whispered those words to myself so many times, believing them. But now, standing there, my body betraying me, my voice stolen, I realized something. I didn't want to die. I didn't want to be taken advantage of. Not like this.

Tia took me upstairs to her dorm room. My body could barely function. My limbs felt like they weren't my own, and I was too weak to fight. I trusted her. I thought she was keeping me safe. But then she left me. And they were still there. I don't remember everything. My mind has mercifully locked away parts of it, but one core memory remains seared into my brain like a scar that will never fade. Hands on me. Heavy. Unfamiliar. Bodies pressing me down in a careless rhythm. Whispers. Laughter. Then darkness swallowing me whole.

When I woke up, my body screamed in pain. Every part of me ached, but the worst of it was between my legs, a sharp, raw soreness that made my stomach turn. And then I saw it—blood. My underwear was stained with it. The sight of it sent a shudder through me, a sickening wave of nausea and horror crashing over me. I forced myself to sit up, to move, to breathe, but every motion made the truth sink in deeper. Something had happened to me.

I turned to Tia, my voice hoarse and shaking. "What ... what happened?"

She wouldn't look at me. She just shrugged and muttered, "You had sex."

Three words. Cold. Casual. Like it was nothing. Like it wasn't stolen from me. My breath caught in my throat. My hands trembled and my skin crawled as I pulled on my clothes. My body didn't feel like mine anymore. I had to get out of there before I shattered into pieces.

"I have to go home," I stated.

Tia barely reacted. She called one of her friends to take me home later that night. No concern, no guilt—just a favor to get rid of me. As I sat in the car, staring out the window at the blur of streetlights, I felt nothing. No tears. No screams. Just emptiness. I didn't tell my parents right away. I couldn't. I was terrified. Terrified of what they would say. Terrified of what they would think. Tia still wouldn't tell me anything. No details. No names. Just vague words that left me spiraling in the dark, grasping at broken memories that didn't make sense. Days passed before I finally broke. I sat in front of my father, my hands clenched into fists so tight my nails cut into my palms.

"Something happened to me," I whispered.

The words barely made it out before I dissolved into sobs. He took me to the hospital, where they did a rape kit, but it was too late. I had waited too long. The evidence was gone. I had nothing. No proof. Just a body that no longer felt like mine and a memory that played over and over again in my head like a horror movie I couldn't turn off. When I got home, my mother's rage exploded.

"I TOLD YOU NOT TO GO!" she screamed. Her voice cracked with something between fury and heartbreak. I stood there silent, her words cutting deeper than any knife ever could. She was right. She had warned me. She had begged me not to go. But what she didn't understand was that I had never been afraid of danger until that moment. I had welcomed it. I had spent so long believing that if I had to die, I wanted my blood on someone else's hands.

But now, staring at my own blood on my underwear, knowing multiple hands had caused it—and yet, I still lived—it made me cringe. The world had taken from me, ripped me apart, but it had left me breathing. And that was the cruelest part of it all. No justice, no closure.

My mother and I spoke to a lawyer, but I knew before she even opened her mouth that there was no hope. No evidence. No names. A popular college campus where a girl like me would always be blamed. I could already hear the whispers: *She was drinking. She was partying. She shouldn't have been there. That's what happens when you out here being fast.* I didn't have the strength to fight, so I walked away with nothing but a single, haunting memory that still plays in my mind like a movie I can never escape.

By nineteen, I was already a ghost in my own life—just a body moving through the motions, hollowed out from the inside. The girl I used to be was long gone, buried beneath the weight of everything that had happened. What remained was someone reckless, someone numb with no sense of direction or purpose. I clung to marijuana like it was my only lifeline, the only thing that dulled the constant ache clawing at my chest. The more I smoked, the further away I drifted from reality, from myself. But it was never enough. The pain still found me in the silence, creeping in through the cracks, whispering in the back of my mind. I didn't want to be here anymore, and still I was too afraid to leave by suicide.

The fear of Hell held me hostage. I had grown up believing that some sins could never be forgiven, that choosing to end my own suffering would damn me forever. So, I stayed trapped in a life I didn't want, in a body that didn't feel like mine. I started fantasizing about ways to make the pain stop without being the one to do it.

So, the deadly cycle continued. I lived recklessly, hoping if I pushed the limits hard enough, the universe would make the decision for me. I took risks that no sane person would. I wandered into dangerous places, placed myself in situations where the odds of survival weren't in my favor. I dared the world to take me out. But every morning, I woke up. Still here. Still breathing. Still waiting for the day when my reckless existence would finally catch up to me.

# Rebellious Soul

In Matthew 13, Jesus tells a parable about four types of soil, comparing a person's heart receiving the gospel to the way a seed responds to different ground. Some seeds take root and flourish. Others are choked by thorns or stolen away. Then there's the seed that falls on rocky ground and never has a chance to grow because it lacks deep roots.

That was me. I wanted to believe, but my faith was shallow, and fragile. The moment life threw storms my way, the little bit of trust I had in God crumbled, swept away like dust in the wind. Instead of leaning on Him, I stumbled further into darkness, searching for something, anything, to fill the growing emptiness inside me.

Then, in 2016, I met Alex. My third relationship I had ever been in, it was extremely toxic. I should have never been with him, but at the time, I didn't see it that way. I was desperate for love. Even though he was an atheist, I convinced myself that I could save him, that my shaky faith could somehow bring him closer to God. What a joke. Instead of pulling him toward the light, I let him drag me deeper into the shadows.

I lost myself. Completely. I stopped caring about God, about myself, about anything that once made me, me. My reflection became unrecognizable. My spirit dulled under the weight of depression.

I turned to smoking, overeating, and numbing myself in every way possible. I told myself I was fine. That I was in control. But the truth was I was falling apart piece by piece, and I had no idea how to stop it.

Alex was Hispanic, and his world was unlike anything I had ever known. Growing up sheltered under my parents' strict rules, I wasn't prepared for the cultural shift. Everything around me felt foreign, as if I had stepped into a life that wasn't meant to be mine. But that was just the beginning. I didn't know it yet, but something was coming. Something that would shake me to my core.

Growing up, I lived in a two-parent household with female siblings, tucked away in a quiet, rural area. Though our family was large, there was a cold distance between us, like we existed in different worlds moving parallel, but never truly connecting. The warmth that should have filled a home was replaced by silence, and I became accustomed to feeling alone despite being surrounded by people.

Everything changed when I left my parents' house and moved to Alex's cousin's place in the heart of the downtown area on the south side of my hometown. It was a world so different from the one I knew. It was raw, gritty, and alive with chaos. The streets pulsed with activity. Crime rates soared, and corners were filled with fiends and dope boys who seemed to claim the streets as their own. It was overwhelming, yet exhilarating in a way I couldn't quite understand.

I watched it all, mesmerized by a lifestyle I had only heard about, but never seen. I found myself drawn to it, caught in a dangerous dance between curiosity and thrill. A part of me secretly craved the rebellion I had never been allowed to experience.

We shared a cramped three-story house packed with three or four families at a time, each one with their own struggles and stories. The walls seemed to breathe with the weight of so many lives pressed together in one space. We smoked, drank, and lost ourselves in the rhythm of Bachata music, letting it fill the gaps in our souls. The beat, the rhythm, the sensuality of the music became our escape, our anthem. In those moments, there were no rules or responsibilities, just a wild freedom that made me both alive and free. There was something intoxicating about the way we lived—like we were dancing through life with no care in the world, even as the shadows of reality loomed just beyond the music's reach.

Moving into a Hispanic household was like stepping into another world—one I didn't know I had been craving. I fell in love with their culture, their traditions, the rhythm of their language, the way their lives felt so alive compared to the quiet, controlled existence I had grown up in. It was all new, but more than that, I fell in love with him.

Alex was in the streets, and the thought of standing by his side slinging dope made my pulse race. There was something thrilling about the danger, the recklessness, the way he seemed to walk through life untouched by fear. He didn't care about consequences. He didn't flinch at the thought of death. He had spent his childhood being beaten down by the world, and now he walked through it like he had nothing left to lose. And I wanted to save him like I wanted someone to save me.

I convinced myself he had potential, that beneath his hardened exterior was a man who could have a beautiful life if only someone believed in him. I wasn't in love with who he was. I was in love with the idea of who he could be. In my mind, we were the perfect couple—untouchable, unstoppable, and just misunderstood. I romanticized everything about him. His sun-kissed bronze skin glowing under the dim lights made me want to reach out just to feel its warmth. His long, thick Puerto Rican hair cascaded down his back, each strand holding a story I longed to unravel. His smile—wild and effortless—could light up the darkest room, and I let myself believe it was meant just for me. And the tattoos—they covered his body like an intricate map of his past. Every line, every design, whispered stories of struggle, survival, and defiance.

He wore his pain like armor, and I admired him for it. There was something magnetic about the way he moved, how he hustled through life with a dangerous charm that both thrilled and terrified me. Whether legal or not, he always found a way to win, and I found myself drawn deeper into his world. I thought I could take the parts of him that excited me and strip away the rest. Mold him into the man I wanted him to be. Heal him. Save him. But in reality, I was the one who needed saving.

Twice—*twice*—God tried to warn me. He laid the red flags right in front of me, clear as day, but I was too blind, too stubborn, too lost in my own destruction to listen. Looking back, I know how this might sound. Maybe you'll think my mind was playing tricks on me, that my addiction blurred reality. But deep in my soul, I believe God will go to unimaginable lengths to pull us back before we unravel completely. Both encounters came while I was lost in the haze of marijuana, my mind drifting between reality and something else entirely.

The first time, I was lying in the small, cramped room we shared. The air was filled with tension I hadn't yet learned to recognize, a silent warning pressing against my chest. As I laid beside Alex in bed, wrapped in the illusion I had created, something happened.

I looked up at the wall, and there He was. Jesus. His face appeared, clear as day, staring back at me with an expression I couldn't shake. His eyes weren't angry, but they

37

weren't soft either. They held something heavier—disappointment. It was as if He was asking me, *Is this really what you want?*

My chest tightened, my breath shallow. I blinked and rubbed my eyes, trying to convince myself it was just the weed playing tricks on me. But deep down, I knew. God was warning me, and yet, I still ignored Him.

On another occasion, I remember the fear gripping me as I watched Alex standing in the kitchen making dinner. His eyes suddenly darkened, and his face contorted in ways that made my blood run cold. In that moment, I tried to reason with myself logically from a sober mind. There's no way he can make his eyes go black like that, no way his face can twist up in such a terrifying way just to scare me. This isn't some prank. Deep down, I knew something far more sinister was happening. It wasn't him. It was something darker, a spirit that had manifested before me. I was so naïve, I told him what I saw and he called me crazy.

Looking back, I now understand that God grants certain people the gift of discernment, the ability to see what others cannot. It is a heightened awareness of the darkness lurking beneath the surface, a spiritual warning of the dangers hidden in plain sight. Some call it intuition, others a gut feeling. But I know now it was God, whispering, "Watch closely. Look deeper. This is not what it seems."

He had been trying to warn me all along, revealing the demons residing in the people around me. The problem was, I wasn't ready to listen. Looking back, I see it so clearly now—Jesus was always there, watching, warning, callingout to me even when I refused to listen. Behind closed doors, in the moments I thought no one could see, He saw me. He saw my pain, my desperation, my reckless pursuit of love in all the wrong places. And He saw Alex—

the man I had bound myself to—as the darkness I was willingly embracing.

Jesus wasn't just showing me my own brokenness; He was exposing the demons I had entangled myself with. The soul ties I was forging with this man were deeper than just physical; they were spiritual, dragging me further into a pit I didn't know how to escape.

The longer I stayed, the worse it got. What started as passion turned to poison. His love was never love at all; it was manipulation wrapped in sweet words, betrayal masked by fleeting moments of affection.

He cheated over and over with girl after girl. Each time, I caught him. Each time, I confronted him, hoping for remorse, for change. But instead of guilt, I was met with rage. He hated being exposed. Hated that his sins were dragged into the light. Hated me for seeing the truth he refused to acknowledge. And with every heated argument, every venomous word he threw my way, I sank deeper into my own torment.

His obsession with pornography grew, feeding his unquenchable hunger for more, for anyone, but me. And with it, my self-worth crumbled. I no longer recognized the girl staring back at me in the mirror. I wasn't enough for him. Maybe I never had been. Maybe I never would be. I stayed— God, I stayed—even as I felt myself unraveling, as the pit beneath me widened, swallowing me whole.

With each heated argument, he became more violent, pushing me against walls, choking me, stomping on me, and kicking me in the stomach. He was smart enough to never hit me in my face. Instead, he threatened to break my arms and dragged me across the floor until I begged him to stop. He would make me constantly eat, hoping I would hate myself and believe no one else would want me. I just wanted to be in a healthy relationship so badly, believing if the relationship was healthy, it would heal me. He would always tell me he would never hurt me again until he discovered I no longer needed to hear those words to stay.

This was only the beginning of our toxic relationship. At the time, I felt I had nowhere to go. I refused to go back home to live with my parents, so I decided the best choice was to stay and make an escape route. It took me three years of working two jobs while going to school to make enough money to buy my own apartment and vehicle. It wasn't much, but it was enough to make me realize the things I worked for could be taken by no one!

When I became financially independent, it finally settled in that I no longer needed him to financially support me. Tables quickly turned and I became the provider of the house. He could never keep a job, and I refused to lose everything I worked so hard for. He had no real home to go back to because his own family no longer wanted anything to do with him. If we ended things for good, he'd be stranded with nowhere to turn. And he made sure I knew it.

He played on my weaknesses, manipulating my deepest wounds to keep me tethered to him. Every fight ended the same way: the silent treatment. He knew how much I hated it, how being ignored tore open old wounds from my childhood—the feeling of being unseen, unheard, misunderstood—and he used it against me like a weapon. I would beg him to speak to me, to just say something so we could fix it. My voice would crack, my pride long gone, as I pleaded for some kind of resolution. But he would stay silent for hours, watching me break, letting me fall apart under the weight of his rejection.

When he had punished me enough—when he had me desperate enough—he would finally acknowledge me, but not with words. With sex. It became our twisted routine. We never fixed anything, never confronted the poison that ate away at us. Instead, we buried it under moments of false intimacy, convincing ourselves that if our bodies could find each other, our hearts would follow. But I knew better. Deep down, I knew we were just drowning together.

I was too afraid to tell my family the depths of the toxicity. I was ashamed. I didn't want them to see how far I had fallen. So instead, I called his mother. When things got really bad, I even reached out to my friends' moms, desperate for someone to pull me out of the wreckage. And they did. For a moment. But I always went back. The trauma bond had me chained to him, a prisoner to the very thing that was destroying me. I kept hoping that if I just loved him harder, he would change. That if I just endured a little longer, we could find peace. But there was no peace between us. I had to look for it somewhere else.

For a long time, I struggled with my faith and ultimately distanced myself from God. While I had experienced moments where I felt His presence—especially in near-death situations where I sensed His intervention—I couldn't reconcile these profound experiences with the absence I felt in the difficult, mundane moments in my everyday life.

My life, at the time, was filled with constant challenges, and I found myself questioning the nature of my relationship with God. How could I continue to believe in a deity who seemed to show up only in life-or-death moments, but was absent in the quiet struggles, the days when I felt overwhelmed, exhausted, or alone? I began to wonder if I was merely relying on God's presence as a form of last resort instead of feeling His guidance and support throughout my everyday journey. The sense of disconnection grew, leading me to question the value of a faith that didn't seem to offer me the comfort and consistency I needed through all of life's ups and downs.

This internal conflict led me to withdraw and abandon my relationship with God. So, I began to seek peace in non-traditional ways.

In 2019, my search for answers led me to a well-known YouTuber whose message captivated me. His videos spoke of unlocking the infinite powers within us to feel truly alive, to transcend limitations, and to become the greatest version of ourselves. The way he articulated personal transformation, the promise of empowerment, and the possibility of living a more purposeful life resonated deeply with me. It felt like I had stumbled upon a path that could finally guide me toward the fulfillment and clarity I had been yearning for.

I was drawn to the idea of tapping into untapped potential, of breaking free from the mental, emotional, and spiritual constraints I had lived with for so long. His words were persuasive, offering a vision of life where limitations could be overcome and personal growth was not only possible, but inevitable. The more I watched, the more I became consumed by the idea that unlocking my inner powers would somehow lead me to a state of enlightenment and success.

Curiosity led me deeper into this world. As I continued to explore the videos and recommendations of this YouTuber, I found myself coming across other creators who delved into similar topics, each offering their own unique perspective on self-empowerment. Some spoke of the Law of Attraction, others of energy healing, meditation, and the ability to manifest one's desires through focused intention. It was a new age of thinking that promised spiritual and personal transformation, and it seemed like a world of possibility was opening up before me.

These new-age practices seemed to offer a sense of control over life and its outcomes, a way to create our own reality through thought and intention. I began to explore these teachings with increasing interest, each practice and belief system drawing me in further, until it felt like I was on the edge of uncovering profound truths that had been hidden from me. For the first time in a long while, I felt like I was part of a movement that could lead to deeper understanding, inner peace, and real change.

But with each step into this world, I found myself slowly drifting away from the foundational beliefs that had passed down from one generation to the next. As these new ideas opened doors to unfamiliar territory, they simultaneously raised new questions and created internal conflict. What began as a quest for personal empowerment began to evolve into something far more complex, leading me down a path where I was both searching for deeper answers and, unbeknownst to me, distancing myself from the very truths I once held dear.

If you aren't familiar with New Age Spirituality, this is a modern-day practice developed in the 1970s by people who wanted to break away from the religious norms. New Age combines elements of various ancient religions into one belief system. It centers on self-development and transformation, with practices like meditation, yoga, tarot card readings, shadow work, and the use of crystals and oils. These practices give the illusion of "aligning" with one's higher self, or "god," to manifest the life one desires. I meditated, burned sage and palo santo to "cleanse" our house of negative energy, and dabbled in tarot readings.

One day, I stumbled across a woman offering tarot readings for just a few dollars in a private Facebook group. Her offer seemed innocent enough—an opportunity to seek clarity, to understand what was hidden in the unseen regarding my current relationship and distant future. I nervously sent her the money, unsure of what to expect.

She asked for a picture of the both of us. I sent the picture, but I didn't want to get my hopes up after paying a random stranger a few dollars to tell me my life story. She returned the photograph with vivid green, yellow, and purple markings all over my face. Each line seemed to pulse with meaning, as though she was mapping out a future only she could see. She wrote to me that I would one day be a successful businesswoman. Her words carried the weight of certainty. She continued, "But he will never be the man you need, and he will never be a good father."

Her words lingered in my mind like the fading afterglow of the colors she painted on my face—bold, unforgiving, and impossible to ignore. That moment never faded from my memory, but I continued to hold onto the broken relationship I had with Alex. I went deeper into New Age practices doing spells, channeling spirits through "angel numbers," and listening to psychics and hypnotists, thinking I could create this foreign reality she spoke about.

At this time in my life, I thought I had my destiny all figured out, and the moment someone mentioned God or the Bible to me, I would immediately get enraged and challenge them on the truth and existence of God. Sadly, I wanted to find the truth, but, like my childhood curiosity, it was as if nobody could give me the answers. I thought the "universe" could align me in life and give me my heart's desires. I thought I could seek God through other ways, but it wasn't so.

I began mixing Christian and pagan practices, not realizing I was perverting the gospel. I was willing to twist scriptures for my worldly desires and would pray prayers from Psalms while using crystals and journaling scripts of how I envisioned my life in the future to become my present reality. I began spreading these perverted truths to family and friends. I had proof my magic worked, so they began to practice it as well.

Desperation makes you do crazy things. I was spiraling, grasping at anything that felt like control, like an escape. That's how I ended up on YouTube, scrolling through spell work tutorials like some lovesick fool. A spell to reconnect with an ex-lover, John, my second relationship in life. Although it had been years since I'd seen him, time didn't erase the way he made me feel. He was my peace once, the calm before the storm I didn't know was coming. And now, drowning in chaos, I wanted to go back. Back to the days when love felt easy, when my heart wasn't as bruised and broken.

There was just one problem—John was married. But in *my* head, I had him first. That was enough to justify it, to convince myself that what we had was unfinished business, not betrayal. I whispered the words of a love spell I found on YouTube and followed the ritual, letting the darkness work its way into my intentions. And whether it was coincidence or something more, it worked.

We met at an out-of-state hotel three hours away, away from prying eyes—away from my toxic relationship with Alex. My heart pounded the entire trip, my thoughts a mess of guilt and anticipation. But the second his hands were on me, reality hit like a slap to the face. This wasn't peace. This wasn't love. This was wrong. Minutes into the act, I shoved him away, my body rejecting what my mind had begged for. I couldn't do it. I *wouldn't* do it. I had spent so long looking for a way out of my pain, but this wasn't it. This was just another trap, another mistake waiting to devour me whole. John, the man I once loved so dearly, was now lying next to me, but I felt nothing. The connection was gone, and the emptiness screamed louder than any pleasure ever could.

And then it hit me even deeper—this wasn't just a personal failure. This was a reflection of a generational curse I had watched tear through my own family. I knew what infidelity could do. I had seen with my own eyes how it shattered homes, how it ripped trust apart, how it left children confused and spouses destroyed. It saddened me to my core that something so destructive had already left its mark on those I loved most. And now, here I was, standing in the same mess, becoming the very thing I once hated. The girl who could be responsible for splitting a household. The girl with no boundaries. The girl who had gone too far.

I hadn't just lost control; I had lost myself. That moment forced me to confront a truth I could no longer deny: I had to stop this cycle. I couldn't carry this pain forward. I couldn't keep making excuses. If I didn't put an end to it now, it would keep repeating, passing from one broken heart to the next.

When I went back home to Alex, I wasn't really there. I walked through the door, but my soul didn't follow. Something inside me had already shut down, like a switch had been flipped, and I knew—I was done. I had spent four years loving this man, fighting for him, losing myself piece by piece just to keep us afloat, but I wasn't willing to drown anymore.

Now, I felt nothing. No anger, no sadness, no love. I wasn't connected to him anymore. I wasn't connected to anything. All I needed was one final push—one last surge of strength—to rip myself away from him completely. To finally set myself free.

A few months later, something shifted inside me. I didn't recognize it at first; I just knew I felt different. Lighter, maybe. Or restless, like a storm was coming, and for once, I wasn't afraid of it. One night, as we stood outside smoking, I turned to Alex. The words came out before I even knew what I would say. "I feel a shift happening in my life. I can't explain it, but I need you to either get with it or I'll have to let you go."

He just smiled that same smug, knowing smile he always gave me when he thought he was ten steps ahead, and said, "I've been preparing you. Getting you ready for your husband."

I stared at him in disbelief. I knew we were toxic. I knew I deserved better. But hearing him say it, as if our years together had just been some kind of training ground for another man, sent a sharp pain through me.

"I want *you* to be my husband," I admitted, my voice barely above a whisper.

He shook his head. No. Just like that. No hesitation. No second thought. Just ... no.

That night, I prayed. I didn't beg for him to stay, didn't plead for love that had already rotted away. Instead, I asked God that if this man was meant to leave my life, let him go peacefully. No fights. No screaming. Just an ending I wouldn't have to dig my way out of.

A month later, the final betrayal came—not another woman, not some explosive argument. No, it was something simple compared to our previous disputes, but it was one boundary I established for myself that I wouldn't dare let anyone cross. I checked my bank account and saw the truth laid out in numbers and transactions. Small purchases scattered over the past few months. Money slipping away without me even noticing. He'd been stealing from me. I had tolerated disrespect. I had endured lies, manipulation, and pain. But this? This was different. This was mine. My hard-earned money, my sacrifices, my security. That was it. The final string snapped.

"You have to leave," I told him, my voice steady. No rage, no heartbreak. Just certainty. I helped him pack his bags quietly I watched him walk out of my life and for the first time in four years, I felt nothing but peace. Not anger. Not sadness. Just a quiet, undeniable knowing. I was finally free from him.

After our toxic relationship ended, I was desperate for healing. I knew I couldn't keep repeating the same cycles, running into the same kind of pain, but I didn't yet know how to truly seek God.

Instead, I turned to what I thought was spirituality—New Age practices, praying to the "universe" for healing, meditating on self-improvement, trying to manifest a better version of myself. I convinced myself that if I just focused on personal growth, I could fix what was broken inside me. So, I made a promise: I wouldn't date again until I had worked through my unresolved trauma. I needed to heal, to find peace within myself, to become whole. Ironically—or rather, divinely—I met my husband a month later.

In 2020, a year marked by uncertainty and global upheaval, I found myself navigating a period of deep introspection, using social media as a means of distraction. The pandemic had reshaped how we interacted with the world, and scrolling through my feed was a way to fill the silence. One day, as I checked my notifications, I noticed a suggestion on Facebook for a person I might know. Since leaving Alex, I promised myself I wouldn't chase after love anymore. I had convinced myself that I needed to focus on healing, not on seeking validation or affection from someone else. But something about this man—his image, his presence, even the small details of his profile—captured my attention. It was as though fate was nudging me to reconsider my vow.

Let me be honest for a moment: when I saw his photo, there was an immediate, almost magnetic pull. He had the kind of physical presence that was impossible to ignore: muscular, with a deep caramel complexion, and a poise that reminded me of a young Dwayne "The Rock" Johnson. In a flash, my vow to myself seemed to vanish. Despite my earlier promise, I found myself considering the decision to send him a friend request. The uncertainty of his sparse profile only added to the intrigue—could he really be who he said he was? Or was this some kind of online deception? Yet something inside urged me to take the leap, to allow myself this small moment of connection.

Within hours, Josh sent me a message—a simple wave emoji. It was disarming, light, and casual. I couldn't help but respond, engaging in a conversation that slowly unfolded over time. As we exchanged messages, I grew more comfortable with him. Eventually, I shared my phone number and we began speaking more directly. The world was isolated, and social interaction had become limited. In the midst of all this, the connection we shared seemed like a safe and harmless escape.

We arranged to meet in person, and when I saw him for the first time, everything changed. It felt surreal, almost like I had crossed some threshold into a reality I hadn't imagined. This was the man I had envisioned as a little girl before my thoughts on true love was twisted by perversion—he was kind, strong, and somehow, just out of reach. He opened the car door for me, held space for me in every conversation, and showed me a level of respect and kindness I hadn't experienced previously. His demeanor was thoughtful and consistent, and his actions spoke volumes. He told me about his life—where he was from, his career, his goals. He was originally from California, had no children, and was deeply passionate about his work.

49

His ambitions were clear, and yet despite all of this, a nagging thought lingered in the back of my mind: Why would someone like Josh want someone like me? I convinced myself I was unworthy, unprepared for someone who seemed to have it all together. But as the days went by, he continued to surprise me—sending me messages filled with encouragement and love, gifting me flowers and my favorite snacks, even giving me a diamond necklace as a reminder of how special I was. His kindness was so consistent that it was hard not to be swept up in it.

As time passed, I found myself spending more time with him, talking every day, and, inevitably, falling for him. Yet, deep within, I was still broken—scarred from past trauma and relationships, unsure of how to trust or accept love. I convinced myself that I had nothing to offer him beyond the fragments of my past. I pushed him away emotionally, thinking I wasn't worthy of this kind of love. I feared that allowing myself to love him would only lead to heartache. Despite the walls I built, he persisted. He spoke of his love for me with sincerity, and though I still resisted, he didn't back down.

However, after a few months, I began noticing changes in his behavior. Small things, like turning off his phone at odd hours or placing it face down, became patterns I couldn't ignore. My intuition began to whisper that something wasn't right. My past experiences—ones filled with betrayal—had taught me to be alert for these signs, but I tried to quiet that inner voice. I convinced myself I was simply projecting my past hurts onto him.

One night, the doubts became too loud to ignore. I gave in to the temptation to check Josh's phone. I knew this was a violation of trust, but something inside me couldn't stop. As I scrolled through his messages, my heart pounded with a mix of fear and dread. And then, I found it. Explicit, intimate messages between him and another woman.

The evidence was undeniable. My world shattered. The man I had come to trust and care for had betrayed me in the worst way. In a surge of anger and heartbreak, I confronted him. I showed him the messages, demanding answers. His response was a mixture of disbelief and regret, but there were no real answers or justification. I was left standing in the cold reality of betrayal.

The following days were filled with pain, confusion, and self-doubt. I had so many questions, but one echoed the loudest: Why do I keep ending up here?

I reached out to the other woman, desperate for clarity. She was brutally honest about her interactions with him. The confirmation stung, but even in my anger, something deeper began to stir inside me—an unsettling realization that I could no longer ignore. Yes, he had broken my trust. Yes, he had made a decision that cut me deeply. But when I looked back at our relationship with unfiltered honesty, I saw my own patterns just as clearly as I saw his betrayal.

I had built walls so high that even when true love tried to enter, I had shut it out. I had let my past define how I viewed love, convinced that closeness equaled vulnerability, and vulnerability led to pain. So, when he reached for me, I pulled away. When he tried to love me, I resisted. When he needed connection, I gave him distance. And now I was here—heartbroken, but also face to face with my own self-sabotage.

The weight of the decision ahead of me was unbearable. Do I stay and fight for this relationship? Or do I walk away and choose myself? The irony of it all was I had given my toxic ex endless chances, enduring his abuse, manipulation, and betrayal, all while convincing myself that he would change. And yet, here I was, struggling to give grace to someone who, despite his mistake, had shown me nothing but love, patience, and regret. That thought wouldn't leave me. It gnawed at me, whispering that maybe this time, my heart wasn't supposed to run. With caution, with therapy, and with an uncertain heart, I chose to stay.

One afternoon, as Josh and I walked through the mall, he led me into a jewelry store, casually asking about what kind of ring I liked. My heart clenched. After everything, was he really thinking about marriage? Still, I entertained the conversation. I picked out a ring, admiring its beauty, but not believing for a second it would ever be mine. He told the jeweler, "I will take that one."

As we got into the car, he pulled the ring from his pocket, his eyes locked with mine. "Jairae, this is a symbol of my love for you. It's a promise that I will never betray you again. I know I've hurt you, and I understand that healing will take time, but this is my commitment to you. I want my actions to prove my words."

Tears burned in my eyes. I had never heard words like that spoken to me with such conviction. I had never had a man fight for my heart, not like this. And for the first time in a long time, I felt something unexpected—hope. It wouldn't be easy. Trust would take time. But for the first time, I believed I had a chance at experiencing true love.

As months passed, something remarkable happened—not just between Josh and me, but within me. His love was different. It was steady. It was patient. It was safe. And the more I allowed myself to accept it, the more I realized I had been starving for this kind of love my entire life. For years, I had convinced myself that love was supposed to be chaotic, that passion meant fighting and making up, that commitment meant enduring pain, that love meant earning someone's affection through struggle.

But Josh didn't require me to struggle. He simply chose me. Night after night, I laid in his arms, my past demons trying to creep their way back in. I would cry over the wounds that still ached, the pain that still lingered. And though Josh never forced his beliefs on me, I could feel it in those moments—he was praying for me. I could feel God's love through him, even when I didn't fully understand it. And slowly, something within me shifted. I began to pray—not to the universe, not to some abstract idea of spirituality—but to God. The real, living, personal God who was patiently waiting for me to surrender.

By April 2021, everything in my life had changed. Josh took me to a park one evening for a photoshoot. The setting sun cast golden hues across the sky, reflecting on the water beside us. As we stood together, he knelt, and time froze. "Will you marry me?"

Tears blurred my vision. I was overwhelmed by a flood of excitement, fear, and joy. Without hesitation, I said, "Yes." But what I didn't fully grasp at that moment was that I wasn't just saying yes to him. I was saying yes to a new life, a new love, a new way of seeing myself.

Months later, in the midst of a chaotic world, we stood in a church and made our vows. But this wasn't just a commitment to each other; it was a commitment to God. Looking back, I now understand what I couldn't fully see then: our marriage was a mirror of my own salvation. Just as I had spent years running from true love, I had also spent years running from God.

I had resisted Him, built walls around my heart, and convinced myself that I had to heal myself before I could come to Him. And just like Josh, God didn't require me to be perfect before choosing me. He just loved me. He pursued me, waited patiently for me, and when I finally surrendered, He welcomed me without hesitation. Ephesians 5:25 says,

"Husbands, love your wives, just as Christ loved the church and gave Himself up for her."

Josh's love for me was a reflection of that verse. When I doubted, he was patient. When I pushed him away, he was steadfast. When I struggled to trust, he proved his love through action.

Isn't that what Jesus does for us? We reject Him. We doubt Him. We run from Him. And yet, He never stops pursuing us. His love isn't based on what we deserve. His love is based on His commitment to us, His desire to redeem us, His willingness to sacrifice for us. My marriage wasn't just about finding love; it was about finding God. As I stood there saying my vows, I unknowingly stepped into a divine covenant. Not just with my husband, but with Christ, Himself. Marriage, when built on the foundation of God, is more than just a union between two people; it's a reflection of His love, His grace, and His redemption.

Looking back, I see now that even though I wasn't fully seeking God, He was still seeking me. Even though I was still praying to the universe, God saw my heart. He saw my longing to be made whole, my desperate need for something real, something greater than myself. And in His mercy, He met me exactly where I was, drawing me closer even when I didn't yet realize it was Him.

I didn't expect to meet someone so soon. I wasn't looking for love, wasn't searching for a relationship. I had convinced myself that I needed years to heal before I could ever think about letting someone in again. But God had a different plan. When my husband entered my life, it was nothing like my past relationships. He didn't try to force himself into my world. He didn't demand that I be "ready." Instead, he became a safe place, a reflection of God's love in human form.

It wasn't just that he treated me better than anyone ever had—it was how he did it. The way he spoke to me with patience, the way he respected my boundaries, the way he showed up consistently. For the first time in my life, I saw what godly love was supposed to look like. And through him, I began to see God differently, too. My prayers changed. My desires changed. My heart softened.

At first, I didn't realize what was happening. But then, one night, I fell to my knees and prayed solely to God. It wasn't a polished, perfect prayer. It wasn't rehearsed or eloquent. It was raw, desperate, broken. "God, if You're real … if You're really there … I don't want to do this alone anymore. I don't want to keep running in circles, chasing healing in all the wrong places. I don't know what I'm doing, but I know I need You."

And for the first time in my life, I felt Him. Not in a loud, dramatic way. Not in the way I expected. But in a stillness, a presence, a knowing that I was no longer alone. God had been setting this up all along. He knew I wasn't ready to surrender completely all at once. He knew I would take baby steps, that I would wrestle with doubt, that I would hesitate. But He also knew my heart was shifting. And because of that shift, He sent me someone to help guide me, someone who would reflect His godly love and change the trajectory of my life forever.

My husband didn't "save" me—God did. But God used him to show me what real love looked like, to remind me that I was worthy of something more than what I had accepted in the past. This was God's grace in action—meeting me exactly where I was, even in my brokenness, even in my confusion, even when I was seeking Him in all the wrong ways. Because that's the kind of God He is. He doesn't wait for us to be perfect before He calls us. He meets us in our mess, in our doubt, in our searching—and He leads us home.

## Interactive Moment:

1. Have you ever found yourself sabotaging love or pushing people away because of past wounds? How has your past shaped the way you receive love today?

2. In what ways have you seen God patiently pursue you, even when you were resistant to Him? Are there areas of your life where you still struggle to fully surrender to His love?

3. How does the love described in Ephesians 5:25— where Christ loves the church with unwavering commitment—challenge or reshape your understanding of what true love should look like in your relationships?

# Filling the Void

The heat rose in my chest, a slow burn that turned into an uncontrollable wildfire. It wasn't supposed to happen like this. I had sat through sermons before, listening to pastors share their interpretations of God, yet nothing had ever provoked me the way this moment had.

A few years ago, I visited my husband's family church, sitting quietly in the pews, half-listening as the guest speaker took the stage. But then he said it—words that sliced through me like a blade: "New Age practices are not of God."

Instantly, my body tensed. My hands clenched into fists. I could feel my pulse hammering in my ears. He's wrong! The thought screamed in my mind, but it wasn't enough to just think it. As soon as we left the church and got into the car, the words exploded from my mouth before I could even process them.

"That's not true!" I spat, my voice shaking with frustration. My husband sat quietly beside me, his hands gripping the wheel, his eyes focused on the road ahead. He didn't argue. He didn't challenge me. He just let me unravel. The silence made it worse.

"You'll have to go to church without me," I snapped. My response to Josh was sharp. "I hope you're okay with that."

A line had been drawn. At the time, I didn't recognize the war happening inside me. I didn't see that my anger wasn't really about the pastor's words—it was about the stronghold I was desperately clinging to, a belief system that had become my safety net. Although I had stood before God a year prior to recite my vows in His presence, I still didn't truly know Him. And anyone who challenged my perception of spirituality? They had hell to pay. But God didn't abandon me in my rebellion. Instead, He did what only He could do: He continued pursuing me.

Months later, a friend invited me to an open discussion at a local church. The topic was life's greatest struggles—relationships, finances, health, grief, and faith. At first, I hesitated. I wasn't looking for another church experience that would make me feel like an outsider, but something nudged me to go. Maybe it was curiosity. Maybe it was divine intervention.

I walked in with walls already built, expecting a surface-level discussion. But the conversation took an unexpected turn. The panelists discussed mental health, and soon, everyone in the room was sharing their lowest moments. The weight of their words settled in the air like a heavy fog. Yet, something was missing. No one was talking about the root of the darkness. No one was offering real solutions for the emptiness we all felt.

Then, it happened. I felt a stirring in my spirit—an unshakable urge to speak. My pulse quickened. I tried to push it down, tried to ignore it, but before I knew it, my hand shot up. All eyes turned to me. With a deep breath, I began to share my experience—how I had spent years trying to climb out of my own pit, how I relied on self-affirmations, the law of attraction, and my own willpower to transform my life. I spoke about the power of our thoughts and words, and how we could manifest our realities. I thought I was offering wisdom. Instead, I was exposing my bondage. Exposed in the House of the Lord.

As soon as I finished speaking, a woman—someone I vaguely recognized—stood from the panel. She locked eyes with me and pointed.

"Stand up," she said. My stomach tightened. I hesitated, looking around, unsure if she was even speaking to me. But then she stepped down from the pulpit, walking directly toward me. When she reached me, she didn't speak right away.

She simply pulled me into a hug. In a soft, yet firm whisper, she said words that sent chills down my spine: "Something has a hold on you, and you have to release it. You cannot leave tonight carrying this burden anymore. It's affecting your relationships. You have a wall up."

My body tensed. How did she know that? The tears came and I collapsed in her arms. My sobs wracking my body as she prayed over me, her voice a steady force against the storm inside me. She called out spirits by name—perversion, witchcraft, deception—commanding them to release their hold. For the first time in my life, I felt the weight of spiritual warfare. A heaviness pressed on my chest, suffocating me. The air in the room shifted with an unseen presence. It was as if fire and angelic power clashed around me. I wanted to let go, but I was afraid.

"I CAN'T!" I screamed, my voice raw. My legs gave out and I fell to the floor. The woman knelt beside me.

"It's up to you," she whispered. "You don't have to carry this another day. But you have to choose to let it go."

I had invited these spirits over the course of my life and I had given them permission to stay. But what I didn't understand in that moment was that they had no authority over me—unless I gave it to them. And I had. God, in all His power, could have forced them to flee, but He is a gentleman. He wouldn't tear down the walls I wasn't ready to surrender, so they stayed. That night, I didn't receive full deliverance. But the spirits were exposed. And once something is exposed, it loses power.

When I got home, I collapsed into my husband's arms, my body drained, my mind spinning. He held me close, whispering prayers over me.

The next morning, I did something different. I curled up in bed, opened my Bible, and played worship music on YouTube. At first, I wasn't sure what to expect. But as I closed my eyes, a deep stillness settled over me. I felt God. Not a distant force. Not an abstract idea. It was really *Him*. His presence wrapped around me, filled every empty space, reached into places I didn't even know needed healing. It was overwhelming, yet gentle. Powerful, yet comforting. And in that moment, I knew. This was the God my ancestors had spoken of. The One who had carried generations before me. The One who had never left me, even when I had turned my back on Him. From that day on, my hunger for God grew.

I had spent so much of my life questioning, doubting, and resisting, but now, I had encountered Him for myself. There was no turning back. God began revealing things to me—truths that shattered my previous understanding. He showed me the unseen battles happening all around us. He entrusted me with spiritual gifts. And He tested my faith. I had prayed for Him to use me, but I hadn't realized what that truly meant. He didn't just want my words; He wanted my heart. He wanted all of me. And so, the journey of surrender began. God had taken what the enemy meant for evil and turned it for good. Now, I walk in the light of that transformation.

# Reflective Questions:

1. Are there any beliefs or practices in your life that you've clung to, even when confronted with truth that challenges them? How do you respond when God begins to expose them?

2. Have you ever experienced a moment where you felt the presence of God in a way you couldn't deny? If not, what might be holding you back from fully encountering Him?

3. In what areas of your life have you unknowingly given the enemy authority? What steps can you take to surrender those strongholds to God and walk in true freedom?

# Claim Your Birthright

This chapter serves as an invitation to walk with Christ. If you're not yet a believer but have heard stories of those who follow Him and feel a desire to become one of His followers, this chapter will offer you insight into what it means to accept His salvation and walk in His ways.

Please know this chapter is optional, and there's no rush to make a decision. If you're not ready to give your life to Christ right now, I encourage you to continue reading and interacting with this book. At the end, you'll have a second opportunity to invite Christ into your life.

There's no pressure to make this choice immediately—the decision is entirely yours. You can revisit this chapter whenever you feel ready, and at the end of the book, God will offer a final call for you to accept His invitation. Take your time, and when the moment is right, the choice will be there for you.

In recent years, I've witnessed a growing number of immigrants arrive in our community. Serving these families has been both a blessing and an eye-opener. Many of them fled from violence, corruption, and devastation in their homelands—only to arrive here and face new barriers: language, paperwork, unfamiliar laws, and the struggle to be seen and treated as equal. It quickly became clear to me how deeply impactful it is to lack something most of us take for granted—citizenship.

Not having the legal birthright of citizenship in the U.S. means doors are often slammed shut. Access to healthcare, stable housing, education, or even the simple peace of living without fear can feel out of reach.

I've seen the exhaustion in their eyes, heard the desperation in their voices, and walked into homes filled with uncertainty. These families aren't asking for a handout—they're just trying to survive. And more than anything, they're trying to belong.

As I witnessed their pain, God opened my eyes to a greater truth: this isn't just a social issue—it's a spiritual parallel. Just as immigrants without citizenship face rejection and barriers, so do many people who have not yet claimed their spiritual birthright through Jesus Christ.

We were all born into a world damaged by sin—a place where pain, injustice, and hardship often rule. And just like those seeking a better life in a new land, we long for something more. A life of peace. Belonging. Purpose. Redemption. But without Jesus, those spiritual doors remain closed.

The Bible tells us that salvation is a birthright freely offered by God to anyone who believes. Yet, like immigrants who hesitate to apply for citizenship because they fear rejection or don't know the way, many of us delay accepting Christ because we feel unworthy, uncertain, or too broken. But Jesus made the path clear: "I am the way and the truth and the life. No one comes to the Father, except through me" (John 14:6).

In the same way that being born in America doesn't automatically grant someone peace, success, or happiness—being born into a Christian household doesn't automatically secure your place in the Kingdom of God. Birthright is not just about where you come from; it's about what you choose to believe and receive.

Think of the story of Esau and Jacob in Genesis 25. Esau, as the firstborn, had the right to his father's blessing and inheritance. But in a moment of desperation, he gave it all up for a bowl of stew. Temporary satisfaction cost him something eternal.

Many of us do the same—we exchange eternal promises for momentary relief. We settle. We sell out. And we don't realize what we've given up until it's too late.

I see this same pattern in the lives of people chasing validation, money, relationships, or quick fixes—trying to fill a void only God can satisfy. We were made for more. Just as immigrants endure long, painful journeys for a chance to belong in a land of promise, we too must be willing to leave behind our old life and pursue the Kingdom of God.

Claiming your spiritual birthright means stepping into the identity God has always had for you. It means understanding that your citizenship is not just earthly—it's heavenly. And the beautiful thing is, unlike earthly systems, God doesn't reject you based on your past, your status, or your worth. Romans 9:26 says, "In the very place where it was said to them, 'You are not my people,' there they will be called children of the living God."

So, ask yourself: if you're willing to fight for freedom, safety, and belonging in this world, are you also willing to pursue the eternal freedom that only comes through Christ?

The battle has already been won on the cross. Our role is simply to receive, believe, and walk boldly into the identity we've been given—not as strangers, but as sons and daughters of the King.

## Interactive Activity:
## A Call to Claim Your Birthright

Are you ready to claim your birthright in God's Kingdom? The decision to accept Jesus Christ as your Savior is the most important choice you will ever make. Just like an immigrant who claims citizenship in a new country, you, too, can claim your place in God's eternal Kingdom through Jesus Christ. If you feel in your heart that it's time to accept this free gift of salvation, I invite you to say this prayer of Salvation:

> *Dear God,*
>
> *I come before You today acknowledging that I am a sinner in need of Your grace and forgiveness. I believe that Jesus Christ is Your Son and that He died for my sins, rose from the dead, and offers me eternal life. I ask You to forgive me for all my wrongdoings and to cleanse my heart. I accept Jesus as my Lord and Savior, and I choose to follow Him with all my heart. Help me to live according to Your will and to walk in the freedom You offer. Thank You for the gift of salvation and for the birthright of eternal life in Your Kingdom.*
>
> *In Jesus' name, I pray.*
>
> *Amen.*

If you prayed this prayer and meant it with all your heart, welcome to the family of God! This is just the beginning of your journey. God has great plans for you, and with His guidance, you can experience peace, joy, and fulfillment in His Kingdom. If you made this decision, I encourage you to find a local church or fellowship group where you can grow in your faith, study the Word of God, and be surrounded by others who can support and encourage you.

Remember, you are now a citizen of Heaven, and your birthright in God's Kingdom is secure. Let this be the beginning of a new chapter in your life, filled with purpose and eternal hope.

# Holiness versus Legalism

Over the past several years, I have meticulously documented nearly every encounter I've had with God—whether through visions that felt more vivid than reality, dreams that carried divine messages, unexpected interactions with strangers that spoke directly to my soul, or the undeniable presence of a still, small whisper guiding me in moments of uncertainty.

With each experience, my faith deepened and my doubts dissolved. I no longer question His existence because I have seen His hand at work in ways that defy coincidence. I can now say, without a shadow of a doubt, that Jesus Christ is real, and His Spirit lives within those who believe.

Many believers—and even non-believers—struggle with the concept of salvation. Early in my walk with Christ, I believed my "ticket to Heaven" was earned by my actions, by what I did for Him. I thought my worth in God's eyes was measured by my obedience, my sacrifices, and my ability to follow religious rules. But over time, I began to witness something deeply troubling: religious trauma passed down from one generation to the next. Have you ever heard someone say they felt like the Bible was beaten into them so much that they no longer wanted anything to do with God? This is what I mean by religious trauma, also known as legalism.

Legalism is when rules become more important than a relationship with God. It places more emphasis on standards than on the Savior, more on laws than on love. For example, my mother attended a Christian school where church attendance wasn't just encouraged—it was demanded. From Sunday to Monday, dawn to dusk, she was immersed in rigid religious teaching. The messages were well-intentioned, but they came with ultimatums. She was told she had to remove her earrings to sing in the choir and wear long skirts daily to prove her modesty. The church had emphasized external appearance and strict rules, but she struggled with having a relationship with Christ. When she became an adult, she walked away from God.

Think about it: if all you've ever known about God is a set of impossible expectations—rules that, once broken, lead to condemnation—it's easy to become disillusioned. Some people don't just walk away from the church; they walk away from God Himself, because to them, it all seems the same.

For the first few years of going to church, I struggled with this. I believed I had to follow a strict set of rules to be accepted by God. I believed my dress, my behavior, and my religious performance determined my salvation. When I began studying the Old Testament and the New Testament, the truth began to unfold before me. In the Old Testament, Moses went to Mount Sinai, where God gave him what we now know as the Mosaic Law—a set of over 400 commandments designed to set the Israelites apart from the nations around them. These laws fell into three categories:

1. Ceremonial Laws – such as tithing, animal sacrifices, and feasts

2. Moral Laws – such as the Ten Commandments

3. Civil Laws – governing everyday life in Israel

Since the Israelites didn't yet have Jesus as the ultimate sacrifice, they had to follow these laws to remain righteous before God. If they failed, they had to offer animal sacrifices and seek forgiveness through a priest. But God, in His mercy, saw that humanity could never fulfill the law completely. So, He sent Jesus Christ to be the ultimate, final sacrifice. Now, righteousness is no longer earned by keeping the law—it is given freely through faith in Jesus Christ. Paul makes this clear in Galatians 3:2–6 when he asks, "Did you receive the Spirit by the works of the law, or by believing what you heard? Are you so foolish? After beginning by means of the Spirit, are you now trying to finish by means of the flesh?"

Even after Jesus' death and resurrection, the Galatians had been deceived into believing they still needed to follow the Mosaic Law to be righteous. But Paul reminded them—and reminds us—that we are made righteous through faith, not through works. The law's purpose wasn't to make people perfect; it was to reveal their need for Christ. It was always meant to point us toward grace.

When I first gave my life to Christ, I was on fire for Him. I wanted to be in His presence every moment. I went to Bible study weekly, fasted every Wednesday, and attended church every Sunday morning and evening. Some nights, I wouldn't get home until eight or nine o'clock. I believed if I missed a church event, I was failing God. I changed my wardrobe, throwing out clothes I deemed "immodest." I distanced myself from friends who didn't seem "holy enough."

On the outside, I looked like the perfect Christian. But on the inside? I felt bitterness, loneliness, and entrapment. What was once a joy became a burden. My relationship with God became a chore. I began to resent church, and for the first time since being saved, I felt distant from God, despite all my efforts to "please" Him. It took me years to realize that I had unknowingly become just like the Pharisees, the religious leaders Jesus constantly rebuked in the Bible. I had prioritized rules over relationship. I thought my performance was more important than His presence.

As I visited different churches, I noticed something strange. I saw people dressed in their Sunday best, singing, praising, shouting, and running around the church. But something felt ... off. God had begun to increase my spiritual discernment, the ability to see beyond what's visible to the human eye. And when I looked at some of these people, I didn't see holiness. I saw envy. I saw jealousy. I saw pride. I saw lust. These people looked the part, but their hearts were far from God.

That's when it hit me: We can dress the part. We can follow the rules. We can say all the right things. And still be spiritually empty. True transformation doesn't start on the outside; it starts on the inside.

God showed me that He wasn't concerned with how "perfect" I looked or how many church services I attended. What He wanted was my heart. He wanted intimacy, not just obedience. As I let go of legalism, some people thought I was backsliding. I stopped wearing dresses all the time. I stopped attending church every single Sunday. I stopped trying to earn God's love. The reality was I was closer to Him than I had ever been because for the first time, I wasn't just following rules—I was following *Him*.

Does this mean obedience and holiness don't matter? Absolutely not. But true holiness is not about outward appearances; it's about a heart fully surrendered to God. When you allow Him to transform your heart, your actions will naturally follow. If you're struggling with religious legalism, I encourage you to put God first. Trust His Spirit to guide you. Don't be afraid to let go of man-made traditions. True freedom is found in Christ alone.

My moments with God allowed me to love Him differently, see life differently, and cherish people more deeply.

Through His presence, I discovered that freedom doesn't come from following rules; it comes from knowing Him. For so long, I tried to live up to man's standards, measuring my worth by religious expectations.

But when I truly sought God Himself, I found the missing piece I had been desperately searching for my entire life. Matthew 6:33 (NIV) says, "But seek first His kingdom and His righteousness, and all these things will be given to you as well."

This scripture became my reality. The more I pursued God's heart, the more I realized everything I longed for—peace, joy, purpose—was found in Him all along. With His warnings, He protected me. With His correction, He refined me. With His love, He healed me. And with His grace, He set me free. For the first time in my life, I was no longer haunted by guilt, shame, or emptiness. The pit that once held me captive in my youth—the constant cycle of striving, failing, and feeling unworthy—was finally gone.

I had been chasing things that could never satisfy, but when I sought God, I found everything I had been missing. And this peace that surpasses all understanding is real. It's unshakable. And it's available to anyone who seeks Him because when you truly encounter God, you will never be the same.

## Reflective Questions:

1.  Have you ever felt like your relationship with God was more about following rules than truly knowing Him? How has that affected your faith journey?

2. In what ways have you experienced—or witnessed—religious legalism? How do you think fo-
   cusing on relationship over rules could change your
   perspective on God?

3. What are some areas in your life where you may still
   be trying to "earn" God's love or approval? How can
   you shift your mindset to fully receive His grace and
   walk in true freedom?

# A Call to Repentance

A few months into my spiritual journey, I came across a sermon by Tiphani Montgomery that changed everything. She spoke about how generational curses delay destinies, keeping people bound in cycles of struggle they were never meant to endure. At that moment, something in my spirit awakened. It was as if I had been walking in the dark, and suddenly, a light illuminated the path before me. This wasn't just an interesting message; it was a revelation.

I had spent years feeling stuck, watching the same patterns repeat in my family—broken relationships, financial struggles, and spiritual stagnation. But now, I saw the spiritual root of it all. It wasn't just bad luck or poor decisions; these were strongholds passed down through generations because of disobedience. Deuteronomy 28 lays it out clearly: when we walk outside of God's will, the consequences don't just affect us; they extend to our descendants.

Verse 18 specifically states, "The fruit of your womb will be cursed." In other words, disobedience carries a generational price. These curses manifest in ways we often don't recognize, such as cycles of addiction, infertility, financial struggles, mental oppression. It suddenly made sense. The battles I had been fighting weren't just mine; they were inherited. I realized then that deliverance requires action. It wasn't enough to recognize the problem—I had to actively break the chains that bound my family. This meant fasting, repenting, and walking in obedience. It meant aligning myself completely with God's word, even when it was uncomfortable.

As I reflected on this, Tiphani had invited viewers to join her in a corporate fast to break generational curses. The timing was too perfect to be a coincidence. Just days prior, I had felt an urgency in my spirit to break every chain holding my family back. I knew I had to do this. But the moment I committed, doubts crept in. *Is fasting really necessary? Maybe I can just pray and see change.* I felt resistance in my spirit— the kind that makes you want to find an easier way. That was when I realized some strongholds can only be broken by fasting and prayer (Mark 9:29).

The fast began on February 1st and included:

- Daily 4 a.m. prayer

- Fasting from food and social media from 6 a.m. to 6 p.m.

- Reading the Bible and Rev. James Solomon's book on breaking curses

That first morning, I nearly missed it. The night before, I had eaten pizza despite knowing I was lactose intolerant. By 3:58 a.m., I was jolted awake by stomach pain right on time for prayer. Even in my reluctance, God made sure I didn't miss what He was doing. That moment confirmed something for me: when you sincerely seek God, He will help you follow through in moments you don't have the strength to do so.

As I prayed and fasted, something began to shift in the spirit. On February 23rd, my coworker Kim approached me, hesitantly saying, "I don't know why, but God told me to ask if you've thought about getting baptized." I froze. Just the night before, I had spent hours talking with my husband's cousin about baptism. And now, someone completely unrelated was confirming what God had already placed in my heart. This is what happens when we walk in obedience. God speaks, and when we listen, He moves in ways we can't explain.

Kim invited me to her church's youth night, and by the end of the service, they offered to baptize me on the spot—at 9 p.m. That kind of spontaneous baptism is rare, but it was clear that God's timing was perfect. I called my husband and asked him to come witness this moment. He arrived in shock, asking, "How did this happen?" I just smiled because I knew this was God completing His work in me.

After my baptism, a domino effect took place. My parents, sisters, and friends began dedicating and rededicating their lives to Christ. It reminded me of Acts 16, where Lydia, after hearing Paul preach, was baptized, and soon after, her entire household followed. God wasn't just working in me; He was using my obedience to shift my entire family's trajectory.

As the fast continued, my dreams became more vivid. They weren't just random thoughts; they were messages. In one dream, I stood on a shed. On the inside of the shed was a casket. As I looked over the land, I saw serpents and crocodiles lurking, waiting to drag me down, but I was safe on the roof. When I woke up, God revealed its meaning: The casket represented my old self dying. The creatures below symbolized the spirits that tried to keep me bound, and me sitting on the roof depicted how God had lifted me above them. It was a confirmation of my deliverance.

Days later, my cousin called. She had been interceding for me and had a vision: "I saw four snakes unwrapping around you. One was black, and the others were brown. And I saw Leviathan smirking at you before turning away."

Leviathan. The spirit of pride, confusion, and division (Job 41). It had been attacking me for years, whispering lies, distorting my thoughts, and keeping me in bondage. But my cousin didn't speak fear; she spoke victory: "No weapon formed against you shall prosper."

Even though I didn't feel free yet, I held onto the truth that I was free. Deliverance isn't about how we feel; it's about standing on what God has declared. For a month, I continued fasting, praying, and pressing into God's presence. Then, one night, I took authority over the enemy and declared God's victory. God simply reminded me again something that has taken you a month to believe could be completed within a day if you truly believe. That day I crushed the head of the serpent. The battle was already won—it just took faith and obedience to unlock what had already been done in the spirit. The chains were broken. The cycles ended. My family's legacy had changed. Looking back, I realize that deliverance doesn't come from passive faith—it comes from active obedience. It requires:

- Repentance: Turning away from anything that separates us from God

- Fasting: Denying the flesh to strengthen the spirit

- Belief: Trusting that what God says is true, even before we see it

God is always ready to deliver us, but are we willing to do what it takes to walk in that freedom? Obedience unlocks breakthrough. Fasting breaks strongholds. Repentance opens the door to deliverance. This journey showed me that true freedom isn't just about being saved; it's about being set free. When you step into that freedom, it doesn't just change your life. It changes generations.

# Interactive Guide:
# A Time to Repent, Fast, and Pray

This guide is designed to help you step into a deeper encounter with God by embracing repentance, committing to a fast, and entering into heartfelt prayer. Use this as a tool to reflect, engage, and act on the transformation God is calling you to experience.

## Step 1: Reflect and Repent

1. **Quiet Your Mind:** Find a quiet place where you can sit undisturbed. Close your eyes and take several deep breaths, inviting God's presence to surround you. I encourage you to go on YouTube and listen to Soaking in God's presence worship instrumentals.

2. **Reflect on Your Journey:** Consider the areas of your life where you have held onto old habits, pride, or self-reliance. Reflect on any strongholds or inherited patterns you feel God has been calling you to break.

3. **Confession and Repentance:** In your journal or out loud, write or say the things you were thinking about in Step 2. Confess to God what you have been holding onto for a very long time that has caused you pain or stagnation in your life.

4. **Commit to Transformation:** Ask God to reveal any hidden areas in your heart that need healing. Invite the Holy Spirit to lead you into true repentance.

## Step 2: Commit to a Fast

1. **Decide on a Fast:** Choose a timeframe that feels manageable. This could be a day, a weekend, or a week. Consider what you will fast from (food, social

media, other distractions) as a way to focus your heart on God.

2. **Set Your Intention:** Write down your purpose for fasting. For example: You can fast to have clarity on a matter that has been hard for you to decide on.

3. **Plan Your Fast:** Schedule specific times for prayer and read scripture during your fast. Find scriptures that align with your topic. For example, if you want clarity, reference scriptures like 1 Corinthians 14:33 or Psalm 143:8. Let these be moments when you intentionally seek God's presence.

## Step 3: Enter into Prayer

1. **Prayer Journal:** Open your journal and write down the scriptures that speak to your heart.

2. **Guided Prayer:** Use the following prayer as a starting point, and then let your own words flow:

*Heavenly Father,*

*As I begin this fast, I come before You with a surrendered heart. I set aside distractions and desires of the flesh to make room for more of You. I'm not doing this for recognition or reward, but to draw closer to You and align my spirit with Your will. Strengthen me, Lord, when I feel weak. Help me to stay focused, rooted in Your Word, and sensitive to Your voice. Let this fast not just be about what I give up, but about what You want to pour in: wisdom, healing, clarity, and deeper intimacy. Refine me through this process. Purify my heart, renew my mind, and shift my perspective. I trust that You'll meet me*

*in the quiet moments and that Your presence
will sustain me. Let this fast be a doorway to
transformation, both in my life and in my relationship with You.*

*In Jesus' name,*
*Amen*

3. **Listen and Write:** After praying, take a few moments to sit in silence. Write down any impressions,
   thoughts, or scriptures that come to mind. Allow
   God's whispers to guide your next steps.

## Final Reflection

Take a moment to review your journal entries from today.
Ask yourself:

- What specific areas in my life need surrendering?

- How can I keep this spirit of repentance alive
  throughout my fast?

- What steps can I take tomorrow to continue walking in obedience to God's word?

May this time of repentance, fasting, and prayer open
your heart to a deeper relationship with God, breaking
the strongholds of the past and setting you free for His eternal purpose.

# Creating a Firm Foundation

In life, everything begins with a foundation—whether it's building a relationship or even our spiritual lives. A solid foundation provides stability, ensuring what we build upon remains strong and enduring. Just as a house needs a strong base to weather the storms of life, our hearts and souls need a firm spiritual foundation to handle the trials, doubts, and uncertainties that come our way.

Before we dive deeper, let's first talk about what it means to create and nurture a firm foundation in our lives. A solid foundation in God isn't just about our beliefs; it's about trust and unwavering faith in Him, especially in challenging times or when we can't see the immediate outcome. It's about holding firm to the promises He has given us and believing in what we do not yet see. Building a solid foundation in Christ is one of the most important things we can do in our spiritual walk. Without a strong base of faith and trust, cracks begin to appear, weakening our ability to withstand life's challenges. But how can we ensure that our foundation remains strong and firm? The Bible provides us with clear wisdom on this:

- **Hebrews 11:1:** "Now faith is confidence in what we hope for and assurance about what we do not see."

- **James 1:6–8:** "But when you ask, you must believe and not doubt, because the one who doubts is like a wave of the sea, blown and tossed by the wind. That person should not expect to receive anything from the Lord. Such a person is double-minded and unstable in all they do."

Faith is the bedrock of a firm foundation. When we trust in God and His promises, we aren't swayed by the uncertainties or the waves of doubt. This kind of faith builds stability in our hearts, allowing us to remain strong, no matter what comes our way. But when we doubt, we create cracks in that foundation, leaving us vulnerable to fear and anxiety.

One evening, as I was traveling with my husband, I glanced at a billboard. The image of a red crack in the foundation caught my eye, and it hit me like a ton of bricks.

The Holy Spirit prompted me to reflect: *What does it mean for something to have a crack in its foundation? What does this mean for my life and my relationship with God?*

As I pondered this question, God revealed something profound. My heart is the foundation where He resides, but over time, I had allowed cracks of doubt, fear, and unbelief to form. These cracks were creating distance between God and me, and they were also affecting my relationships with others. In those moments of reflection, God began to gently show me how my lack of faith and trust in Him were contributing to the cracks in my spiritual foundation. It was through this realization that I saw how essential it is to keep our hearts aligned with God's promises, trusting Him even when life doesn't make sense.

It's easy to think trials and challenges are obstacles that should be avoided, but the reality is that they are inevitable. Everyone faces them, big or small. The beauty of walking with God is no matter how unstable life becomes, He remains our rock. I couldn't help but think of the lyrics from Maverick City's song, *Rain Came Wind Blew, But My House*

*Was Built on You.* This reminded me of the importance of having a firm foundation in Christ. What happens when we don't have this foundation? What happens when doubt creeps in and cracks form in our trust in God?

A foundation without trust is bound to crumble. When we face life's storms, if we are not rooted in faith, we will struggle to stand. But with God as our firm foundation, we can withstand the fiercest winds, knowing He's with us.

So, how do we fix the cracks in our spiritual foundation? The good news is it's not as complicated as we might think. It starts with making a choice to surrender our doubts and fears to God, trusting that He has the power to heal and restore. Here are a few steps to begin:

1. **Never depend on your own understanding.** Proverbs 3:5–6 reminds us to trust in the Lord with all our heart and lean not on our own understanding. When we try to control every situation, we create cracks in our faith. Instead, we need to rely on God's wisdom and guidance.

2. **Don't worry about anything.** Worrying weakens our trust in God. Philippians 4:6–7 teaches us to bring our concerns to God in prayer, and His peace will guard our hearts and minds.

3. **Exercise your faith.** Faith is like a muscle that needs to be exercised. The more we trust God, the stronger our faith becomes. Every time we choose to believe in what we cannot see, we build a stronger foundation for our lives.

After deep reflection that evening with God, I felt I had made progress—until I went to bed. I began to feel the oppressive presence of the enemy, filling my mind with anxiety. Fear threatened to overwhelm me. But then, the Holy Spirit reminded me I had the authority to overcome this fear. In that moment, I began to declare the blood of Jesus over my life. As I did, I could feel the spiritual atmosphere shift. I prayed for protection and guidance, and I sensed the power of God's presence driving away the enemy's attacks.

The battle wasn't mine to fight alone. It was God's. When engaging in spiritual warfare, it's essential to recognize that the enemy will use our doubts, fears, and weaknesses to undermine our faith. But we have the power and authority in Christ to stand firm. Here are a few practical steps for combatting spiritual warfare:

1. **Declare the Word of God:** The Bible is our sword. In moments of fear or doubt, speak out scriptures of truth over your life. For instance, say aloud, "I am more than a conqueror through Christ" (Romans 8:37), or "No weapon formed against me will prosper" (Isaiah 54:17).

2. **Pray for Protection:** Always invite God's protection into your life. Psalm 91 is a powerful prayer of safety and refuge, reminding us that God will protect us from the snares of the enemy.

3. **Resist the Enemy:** James 4:7 says, "Submit yourselves, then, to God. Resist the devil, and he will flee from you." We don't need to be passive in the fight; we actively resist the enemy's attacks by standing firm in God's truth.

4. **Worship:** Praise and worship are powerful weapons in spiritual warfare. When we lift our voices in worship, we invite God's presence to drive out darkness. As Psalm 22:3 says, "God inhabits the praises of His people."

In every battle, remind yourself of your identity in Christ and the authority you have through Him. If you struggle with anxiety or doubts, I encourage you to reflect on the wisdom of Luke 12:22–31, which reminds us that worrying can't change anything. God provides for the birds of the air. How much more will He care for you? Let these words bring peace to your heart and strengthen your trust in His provision. When battling anxiety, speak over yourself that God is in control. Reaffirm that you don't need to carry the weight of the world because God's peace is greater than all understanding. (Philippians 4:7)

# Interactive Reflection: Strengthening Your Foundation

Take a few moments now to reflect on the moments in your life when you've experienced God's faithfulness. Perhaps it was a financial breakthrough, healing, or the restoration of a relationship. Write down one or two of these moments.

# Reflection Questions:

- How did God show up for you in a situation where you thought there was no way out?
- What did you learn about God's ability to provide and guide you?

These reflections will serve as powerful reminders of God's unwavering faithfulness, helping to strengthen your trust in Him.

Building a firm foundation in God requires trust, surrender, and an unwavering belief in His goodness. As we continue to strengthen our faith, we can rest assured that God will always be our rock. No matter how fierce the storm, if we are rooted in Him, we will not be shaken. Remember, God desires to strengthen your foundation. By trusting in

Him and exercising faith, you will create a foundation that won't crack under pressure. Even in the hardest of times, He is with you every step of the way.

# Scriptures for Reflection:

1. Hebrews 11:1
2. James 1:6–8
3. Romans 8:37
4. Isaiah 54:17
5. Philippians 4:6–7

They say the teacher doesn't give the test for their own benefit, but for the growth of the student—for the student to gain knowledge, endurance, and wisdom they can carry for a lifetime.

That's exactly what God did with me. He didn't test me to break me; He tested me to build me. He began by teaching me what it meant to have a firm foundation in Him. Not just in word, but in experience. He stripped away the surface-level comfort and dug deep into the soil of my soul, teaching me how to anchor myself in His truth, His presence, and His promises—even when nothing made sense.

Then, without warning, He took me on a journey, a three-year stretch that felt like walking blindfolded in the dark to chase a promise I couldn't see, touch, or explain. It was uncomfortable. It was lonely. But it was necessary. Because God wasn't just preparing me for the promise; He was preparing the promise for me.

What I didn't understand then, I see clearly now: the test wasn't punishment. It was preparation. Every delay, every detour, every moment I wanted to quit was part of the process that shaped me into who I needed to be to receive what He had already written for me. Faith doesn't always look like shouting in church. Sometimes it looks like staying when you don't understand. Trusting when you can't trace Him. Believing when nothing around you confirms the promise.

And that's what I did. I stood on the foundation He taught me to build. And step by step, that invisible promise started becoming visible. Life has a way of pushing us to our breaking points, testing our strength in ways we never imagined. There are seasons when the weight of uncertainty feels unbearable, and we're forced to confront the deepest parts of ourselves—the fears, the pride, the impatience, and the doubts we thought we had long outgrown.

This has been one of those seasons for me. It's been a season of wrestling with the unknown, a season of sacrifice, and most of all, a season of painful, but necessary growth. Through it all, I've learned the true meaning of trust. Not just the easy, surface-level trust when things are going well, but the deeper kind that holds on, even when everything feels like it's falling apart.

Most importantly, I've learned that God's faithfulness doesn't depend on my understanding, but on His sovereign will. It all began with a promise, an almost impossible dream spoken into our lives by God's voice. My husband and I had dreamed of owning our own home, but for years, it felt like a distant hope. Our financial struggles were constant, and no matter how hard we tried, it always seemed out of reach. I can still remember the sting of rejection after rejection. My credit was stuck in the low 500s, and every application ended with a door slammed shut in my face.

I remember the crushing feeling of hearing a family member say, "Delay is not denial." At the time, I didn't understand those words, but now, I see them for what they were. God was working in the delay. His timing wasn't mine.

His ways weren't my ways. I had to wrestle with the reality that just because something wasn't happening on my timeline didn't mean it wasn't coming. I had to trust that, even in the waiting, He was working behind the scenes, weaving together something far better than I could imagine.

When the promise began to take shape, it wasn't without fear. We were still struggling. No savings. Poor credit. A financial mess that seemed impossible to overcome. Yet, something deep within me stirred, a whisper that urged us to step forward, to move in faith. But even then, doubt crept in. I wanted the house. I prayed for it. But deep down, I knew we weren't ready.

Faith isn't just about belief. It's about action. It's about stepping forward in partnership with God, even when the path ahead is unclear, even when every step feels uncertain. And so, we began. We met with realtors. We toured homes. We spoke with lenders. But with each step, the weight of doubt grew heavier. Why wasn't it happening faster? Why couldn't I just have what I wanted?

In a world that demands instant results, waiting felt unbearable. But this wasn't just about a house; it was about learning to trust God's plan and timing. Every decision, every move had to be made in His direction. And as our lease deadline moved closer, the pressure grew, desperation clouded my judgment.

We found a house. It wasn't perfect, but it felt like our only chance. The pull to act was overwhelming. Yet, in the quiet of my heart, I heard God's still, small voice: *Don't settle. Wait.* It didn't make sense. I felt the pressure to act. The fear of missing out was suffocating. But in that moment, I knew deep within my soul that I couldn't ignore that voice.

We visited the house, and as I stepped through the door, a physical unease swept over me. My spirit screamed, *This is not it*! As we walked through, I found a small pocket

Bible and a box that resembled a miniature casket. The heaviness of the moment settled in. I knew it was time to walk away and this desperate decision would be the death of me. I couldn't explain it, but I told my husband, "We need to leave." He didn't understand, but I couldn't ignore the turmoil within me. The weight of fear and the pressure to make a decision felt suffocating, but deep down, I knew this was God guiding us.

That night, I prayed a simple prayer: "God, if this is not Your will, please make sure we're denied for the loan." The very next day, we were. The relief was almost too much to bear. But then fear crept in. Was this failure? Had we missed our chance? Had all of our efforts been in vain? Yet, in the midst of my fear, God's faithfulness was clear. He was still working, even when I couldn't see it.

That night, my husband dreamt we were in our apartment, and suddenly, gnats appeared, swirling around us. They formed into a hand, guiding me out of the apartment toward the house we had considered. It was strange. It was unsettling. But it was a sign. A sign that we had been acting out of fear, not faith. And God, in His mercy, was guiding us away from a desperate decision.

We surrendered. We let go. We stopped forcing things, and only then did we begin to see God move. But it wasn't easy. In the months that followed, God called us to make difficult decisions. We had to let go of our possessions—my car, my husband's car, our home. We moved in with my sister, and it was a humbling experience. The pride inside me fought at every turn. What would people think? But as we obeyed, I began to understand the depth of surrender. And though it was painful, I saw how it softened my heart, preparing me for what was to come.

Then, things started to change. My husband was promoted at work and received a leadership role and a significant pay raise. We started paying off debts, helping our family, and investing in our future. Slowly, but surely, the fruits of our obedience began to show. The waiting—though excruciating—was starting to make sense.

But God wasn't finished. He called me to step out of my job to take a leap of faith into something new. It didn't make sense financially. It was a pay cut. But there was peace—peace that surpassed all understanding. I knew this was the path God had for me. Looking back now, I can see how every sacrifice, every moment of waiting, was part of something much bigger than I understood at the time. Faith is active. It's trusting God when the road is long, when the journey feels like it might break you. It's knowing that even in the waiting, He orchestrates every detail.

Today, I live in that four-bedroom house—a dream I thought was impossible. But I've gained more than just a house. I've gained a deeper trust in God's plan. I've gained the freedom to follow my calling, to express myself through art, to advocate for my community, and to become the woman God always intended me to be. I'm still waiting on other promises, but I've learned to trust the process. I've learned that when we surrender our will to God, He is faithful to deliver. Even when the waiting seems endless, the harvest is coming.

## Interactive Activity:

Take a moment to reflect on the promises God has made to you. Are there areas where you're struggling to surrender your will to His? Write them down and pray over them. Ask God to reveal His timing and give you the strength to trust Him fully.

Then, take one step of obedience. What action can you take today to partner with God in His plans for you? Whether it's letting go of something, making a decision, or simply waiting with faith, trust that God will guide you every step of the way.

Remember: God is faithful. Even in the waiting, He's working.

# Spiritual Veil Lifted

There's a stark contrast between the practices of witch-craft and divination and the true, transformative power that comes from the Holy Spirit. I spent many years walking in the dark, completely unaware of the spiritual trap I had fallen into. My life was filled with a desperate search for knowledge from sources that seemed powerful, but little did I know I was unknowingly opening doors to spiritual decep-tion. It wasn't until I gave my life to Christ that I understood the difference. Let me share my journey with you and how God revealed the truth about spiritual gifts and the dangers of dabbling in the enemy's territory.

For a long time, I was fascinated by clairvoyance and psychic abilities. These practices promised me insight into hidden knowledge and the future. Clairvoyance—seeing things far away—and clairsentience—feeling the emotions of others—once seemed like gifts to me. I thought I was tapped into something extraordinary, but I now realize those were dangerous practices that invited spiritual dark-ness into my life. These so-called gifts, as the world defines them, are often linked to witchcraft, occultism, and sorcery, methods people use to tap into the spiritual realm through ungodly techniques.

When I surrendered my life to Christ, the Holy Spirit opened my eyes to the truth. As I began to pray and seek God, the deeper I understood that these practices weren't the gifts God had intended for me. The Bible clearly warns in Deuteronomy 18:10–12 against engaging in sorcery, divination, and seeking mediums. These things open the door for demonic forces to manipulate your life. Psychic readings, witchcraft, and astral projection may offer temporary glimpses of knowledge, but they come with a great spiritual cost, often without you realizing darkness taking root in your life.

In this image, you'll see me performing an egg cleanse ritual a few years ago. This was my experience with Brujería, also known as witchcraft, a practice rooted in Mexican American culture. It was my first and last time engaging in such a ritual, as what I saw in the cup—a face and a skeleton—deeply unsettled me. I share this with you not to incite fear, but to show how easily something seemingly innocent, like kitchen cups and food, can be used in practices that delve into the occult.

What I experienced was just the beginning of what witchcraft can involve. Imagine the depths it can reach for someone willing to explore darker forces. Many Christians may not fully understand how real or powerful these practices can be, or they may be afraid to confront them.

However, I want to reassure you that no form of witchcraft, no matter how dark it may seem, is strong enough to stand against the kingdom of God, especially when you have the right people trained to dismantle such demonic forces.

When I was baptized and filled with the Holy Spirit, everything changed. I no longer needed to rely on worldly practices. The Holy Spirit gave me direct access to the spiritual realm, and suddenly, I realized I didn't need to use deceitful, harmful techniques anymore. As I continued to seek God through prayer and fasting, He began to elevate me spiritually. I moved into realms of light, not darkness, and began to witness angelic beings.

God gave me the authority to battle in the spiritual realm for the territories He was calling me to claim. This experience was unlike anything I had encountered in my past practices. It was powerful, exhilarating, and, most importantly, peaceful. I was able to receive messages from God to encourage and warn others. I also began to understand that what I had been experiencing as a child—being drawn to certain places—was God planting seeds of prophecy in my heart long before I understood it. The very building that had intrigued me as a child became a place where I would later serve my community, fulfilling God's purpose for my life.

But even as I began to walk in these new gifts, the journey wasn't without challenges. One night, as I was listening to worship music and basking in God's presence, I was overwhelmed with a profound sense of peace. But suddenly, I woke up feeling drained, as though something was holding me down. When I turned to face the window, I saw two shadowy figures in the corner of my room and a massive black dog standing beside them. I tried to pray, but my body felt too weak to move. I closed my eyes, whispered a prayer for protection, and went back to sleep.

The next morning, I shared my experience with my husband, but he dismissed it as sleep paralysis. I knew what I had seen was real, so I prayed that God would open his spiritual eyes. The very next day, he came to me, stunned, telling me he had heard voices coming from the apartment below us—a strange and unsettling occurrence—and that he, too, had seen the shadowy figures I had described. I knew this was God's answer to my prayer, opening his eyes to the spiritual realm as well.

This was a clear sign that the enemy wasn't pleased with my transformation. In today's world, some people may know these figures to be "monitoring spirits," demonic beings assigned to watch over and sabotage your life. They were demonic forces seeking to block my spiritual gifts and hinder my calling. I realized they were aware of the spiritual gifts God had placed within me, and were trying to interfere with the mission God had given me. But God was faithful. He revealed the enemy's plans before they could take root.

I learned that just as God has angels to protect His kingdom, the enemy also deploys his own forces—watchers of darkness—to guard his territory. However, these forces were powerless against the authority I had through Christ. Through this experience, I began to learn more about the gifts of the Holy Spirit. Ephesians 4:11 speaks of the five-fold ministry: apostles, prophets, evangelists, pastors, and teachers. While some might argue that prophets no longer exist today, I can speak from experience—they do. My prophetic gift has been with me for as long as I can remember; I was just unaware of the gift due to the enemy infiltrating my mind.

As a child, I often saw and sensed things others couldn't understand. I had vivid dreams of tragic events, like seeing my entire family perish in a car accident. But every time, God protected me, waking me up just before the crash. Recently, I shared these childhood dreams with my siblings, and to my surprise, they revealed they'd had the same recurring dreams. The enemy had tried to sow fear and division among us, but now, through God's guidance, I see the bigger picture. The Devil wanted to scatter and destroy us, but God is uniting us to fight against his schemes. We're now walking in our spiritual gifts, understanding our true identity in Christ, and no longer allowing the enemy to deceive us. I now understand that vehicles in dreams often represent the journey toward our destiny. The enemy used fear to try to derail us from God's purpose for our lives.

On another occasion, I experienced paranormal activity that caused objects to move. One morning, I woke up to find that the cross pendant my mother had given me for my twenty-fifth birthday was gone. The chain was still intact, but the pendant had vanished. Just the night before, I had worn it, and now it was nowhere to be found. I immediately assumed it had fallen off earlier that day while I was at the park. But there was no logical explanation. How could the pendant come off without the chain breaking, too? I searched frantically around the house, my heart racing, until I finally spotted it on my husband's side of the bed. A wave of relief washed over me. I thanked God and quickly put the necklace back on before heading to work.

Then, my husband called to tell me he had just received a huge promotion. The joy in his voice was unmistakable, and I couldn't help but thank God for the blessings. In that moment, I wondered if the missing pendant had been a sign, a response to his prayers, a strange confirmation of God's favor. But little did I know, the strange occurrences were far from over.

Three nights later, I woke up suddenly at 2:20 a.m. I sat up in bed, heart pounding. I grabbed my Bible and began reading scriptures, praying for God's protection over everyone connected to me, asking Him to remain at the center of my marriage. The peace that followed seemed to confirm my prayers, but little did I know, something else was about to shake me again.

Later that morning, my husband called and asked if I was missing anything. I confidently said no, only to have him persist.

"What about your promise ring?" he asked. That's when it hit me—I had no idea where it was. He told me it was lying in the middle of our bed. Panic gripped my chest. Was this God trying to communicate with me, or was it something more sinister? I had never experienced objects moving like this—only seen it in movies. I didn't know what to make of it, so I prayed about it and turned to my sisters in Christ for guidance.

In my prayers, I felt led to read 1 John 2:26–27, which says, "I am writing these things to you about those who are trying to lead you astray. As for you, the anointing you received from Him remains in you, and you do not need anyone to teach you. But as His anointing teaches you about all things, and as that anointing is real, not counterfeit—just as it has taught you, remain in Him."

It hit me hard. These strange occurrences weren't signs from God. They were distractions designed by the enemy to confuse me, to make me question my faith, and to lead me away from hearing God's voice clearly. I had been struggling in recent months, unable to discern His guidance, because I had neglected the spiritual disciplines—prayer, worship, and reading the Word—that kept me grounded. My lack of connection to God had allowed the enemy to take advantage of my mind, turning it into a battleground. Looking back, I realize it wasn't just about lost jewelry; it was spiritual warfare in plain sight.

In those moments when my cross necklace and promise ring went missing, I should have recognized the signs. The enemy wasn't just after objects; he was after meaning. That cross around my neck wasn't just decoration, it was a declaration. It symbolized my identity, my covering, and my

95

unshakable foundation in Christ. And when it disappeared, it was as if the enemy was trying to whisper, "I can take that from you."

Then came the promise ring, a symbol not just of my future with my husband, but of a deeper covenant between me and God. It represented more than love; it was a vow of purity, purpose, and obedience. A sacred commitment to walk in alignment with His will.

Yet, gone. Stolen. Just like that. It wasn't coincidence. It was calculated. A spiritual attack designed to make me question my standing with God, to sever my sense of connection and commitment. What felt like simple loss was actually prophetic. The enemy attempted to rob me of the symbols of my faith, hoping I wouldn't notice that the physical theft mirrored a deeper spiritual assault. But here's what I've learned: you can take the symbol, but you can't steal the seal. The cross may have been taken from my neck, but Christ still reigns in my heart. The ring may be gone, but my covenant with God is eternal, written not in silver or gold, but in blood and grace.

What the enemy used to try and break me, God used to awaken me. He reminded me that my authority doesn't come from the things I wear, it comes from the One I walk with. That's the power of having a strong foundation. God can call us to seasons of isolation to prepare and communicate with us more intimately, but the enemy uses isolation differently. He exploits it, twisting it into something that harms our mental and emotional health, leading us into temptation. Without community, we lose accountability. Iron sharpens iron, as Proverbs 27:17 says.

The enemy, like the false prophets of old, will always try to throw us off course. But the Holy Spirit is our guide, and He will teach us, protecting us from the lies that seek to pull us away from the truth. In the last days, there will be deception on every side. Matthew 24:24 warns, "For false messiahs and false prophets will appear and perform great signs and wonders to deceive, if possible, even the elect." The Holy Spirit is our safeguard in these times. Whenever something doesn't align with Scripture, whenever it feels off, we must turn to the Word. If it contradicts the truth of God, it's not from Him. Stay rooted in His Word, and let the Holy Spirit guide you through the confusion, separating truth from error.

Once I prayed about my spiritual sight, the fog of distorted life lifted, finally removing a veil that had been clouding my vision for so long. One moment, everything felt like it was shrouded in confusion and doubt, and the next, the world around me became clearer, brighter, more vibrant than I had ever known. I remember the moment vividly, almost as if time stood still. It wasn't an instant realization, but more like a gradual unfolding, like the pages of a book slowly revealing a story I had always known but couldn't quite grasp.

God, in His infinite grace, reached down and touched my heart. I could feel His presence more profoundly than I ever had before, and in that sacred moment, I knew He was the one who had lifted the veil from my eyes. It wasn't just a physical awakening, but a spiritual one. I saw truth where I once saw only shadows, and the deeper meaning behind everything—the struggles, the joys, the people in my life— became apparent.

Suddenly, I could perceive things I had never noticed: the subtle connections between people, the divine purpose in every circumstance, and the unspoken whispers of love and hope that God places in our lives every day. It was as though I had been walking in a dream, and now, I had awoken to a new reality—one filled with clarity, purpose, and a deep, unwavering peace that I had never known before. This spiritual moment wasn't about gaining new knowledge; it was about seeing with new eyes, eyes that were no longer blinded by the enemy's distractions and confusion of the world.

God had pulled back the veil, allowing me to see the truth of His love and His plan in a way that changed everything. I knew my life would never be the same again. Joel 2:28–29 states, "And afterward, I will pour out my Spirit on all people. Your sons and daughters will prophesy, your old men will dream dreams, your young men will see visions. Even on my servants, both men and women, I will pour out my Spirit in those days."

This scripture reflects God's promise to empower His people with spiritual insight. The Holy Spirit would be poured out on all, revealing His presence and plans, and enabling His followers to discern the unseen, including the schemes of the enemy. After years of being bound by darkness, I encountered this promise in a real and personal way. For over twenty years, I lived in bondage, trapped by tormenting forces in my mind and spirit. But through persistent prayer and a genuine desire to be set free, God delivered me. The Holy Spirit came to reside in me, and I began asking God to reveal my spiritual gifts and uncover what was hidden.

Through prayer, I sought to see into the spiritual realm, and soon, my prayers were answered. Once my spiritual eyes were opened, I experienced a profound shift. Although I had been through immense trauma—molestation, suicidal thoughts, addiction, promiscuity, abuse, mental illness, and even witchcraft that blinded me—God lifted the veil to show me what true freedom is like with him. As I began sharing my testimony in front of crowds, from my past to my present, I felt an incredible weight lift from my shoulders.

The burdens I carried were released, but, as I soon discovered, the battle wasn't over.

Though I had been delivered, something remained. I went home, only to feel a dark presence surrounding me, like a cloud of darkness settling over me. It was as though the very darkness I had surrendered to God wanted to re-enter and reclaim what it had lost.

Matthew 12:43–45 warns, "When an unclean spirit comes out of a person, it passes through waterless places seeking rest but finds none. Then it says, 'I will return to the house I left.' When it arrives, it finds the house unoccupied, swept clean, and put in order. Then it goes and takes with it seven other spirits more wicked than itself, and they go in and live there. And the final condition of that person is worse than the first."

At the time, I didn't understand fully what was happening, but I now realize the enemy wanted to regain control over me. The spirits that had once tormented me grew furious when they saw they could no longer bind me. As I stepped out of the house of the Lord, they attacked my emotions, making me feel angry, upset, and isolated.

Have you ever experienced a moment when it felt like the darkness you surrendered to God was trying to return? The enemy can often attack through emotions, old patterns, or even relationships. It's important to stay vigilant, filled with God's Spirit, and resistant to these attempts to reclaim what God has set free.

As I wrestled with these emotions, I began to see the patterns from my past. I started picking fights with my husband, trying to argue and manipulate, as I had done in previous relationships. My trauma, rejection, and anger were conditioning me to respond in unhealthy ways. But, unlike before, my husband didn't engage. He walked away from the conflict, providing me with the space I needed to confront my own inner turmoil.

I realized the enemy used anger to try to wedge itself between my husband and me. As we argued, I felt the pull of malice, an urge to push him away and focus on everything that wasn't going right.

On another occasion, my husband—whom I knew to be gentle and soft-spoken—seemed distant, more stern than I'd ever seen him. He told me he was tired from the emotional toll of our arguments. I hadn't realized how much the spiritual attack had worn us down. The enemy's goal was simple: divide and conquer. If I could create enough discord, he could break our unity.

That night, as the argument escalated and I began to entertain the thought of divorce, I felt something deeply unsettling in my spirit. I couldn't shake the feeling that something was wrong. This was my wake-up call. God was warning me.

Right before work, I had a vision that my husband and I were driving and were involved in a horrific accident. In that moment, time slowed down. I watched my husband's face hit the steering wheel, and everything seemed to come to a standstill. My heart was gripped with fear. God had revealed something profound: He had given me the vision to show me how the enemy sought to destroy my husband to prevent me from fulfilling my destiny and calling.

The vision wasn't just a warning of danger, but also a reminder of the importance of prayer. As we fight spiritual battles, sometimes we don't know the words, but the Holy Spirit intercedes on our behalf. Remember Romans 8:26: "In the same way, the Spirit helps us in our weakness. We do not know what we ought to pray for, but the Spirit Himself intercedes for us through wordless groans."

God showed me that prayer isn't just about asking for things; it's about actively engaging in battle against the forces of darkness. I knew then that the enemy wanted to destroy my marriage, and I had to rise up in prayer to defend it. Ephesians 4:26–27 reminds us: "In your anger, do not sin. Do not let the sun go down while you are still angry, and do not give the devil a foothold."

I realized I had been giving the enemy access by holding onto anger instead of choosing peace and reconciliation. The vision continued to unfold. The truck he drove symbolized our destiny—a massive, powerful vehicle, capable of great things. But like a truck driver, we had to navigate carefully. We were on a journey, and the enemy tried to throw distractions and obstacles in our way.

God was showing me that the gifts we carry are powerful, but they require training and wisdom to navigate well. The truck's movement, my attempt to put on my seatbelt, and even the way time slowed down all represented the mercy and time God gives us to correct our course. He allows us to make things right, to choose peace, and to embrace love even when we fail. In my vision, I also saw myself holding my husband's head after the crash. This symbolized my role to protect, to love, and to care for him.

My trauma had impacted him, and I had to be aware of how my actions affected him. Jesus commanded us to love one another as He has loved us. But love isn't always easy; it requires effort, patience, and understanding. It also means knowing when to protect, when to comfort, and when to forgive. The way I had been living, allowing trauma and anger to dictate my actions was leading me down a path of destruction. But God's mercy was evident; He helped me realize my choices affected not just me, but also my husband, who was walking through this battle with me. As I embraced these lessons, I began to see the importance of unity, peace, and spiritual vigilance. The enemy seeks to destroy, but God is always there to protect, guide, and heal.

Through prayer, repentance, and love, I found my way back to a place of peace. Your journey toward spiritual insight may involve moments of challenge and vulnerability, but it also holds the promise of deep transformation. God's Holy Spirit is available to help you discern the unseen and protect you from the enemy's schemes. When you surrender your life to Him, He will reveal His truth and provide the strength to resist the attacks of the enemy.

Through prayer, awareness, and vigilance, you can walk in the freedom God has given you. Ask the Holy Spirit to reveal any areas of your life where the enemy might be gaining a foothold. Commit to walking in the light and truth of God's Word, trusting that He will guide you and protect you from every attack. Your spiritual insight is a powerful tool, and with God's guidance, you'll be able to see through the schemes of the enemy and walk in victory.

We often don't realize the enemy can't just take control of us without our consent. Did you know the moment we entertain sin, even in the form of anger or bitterness, we create a space for the enemy to creep into our hearts? Think about that. Is there something in your life right now that's causing division between you and others, or even between you and God?

In closing, I urge you to discern the difference between the counterfeit gifts of the enemy and the true gifts God offers. The world may offer false power, but it comes at a steep price. When you submit to God, He opens your eyes to a higher realm of authority through the Holy Spirit. You don't need to turn to psychic readings or witchcraft to find answers. Through prayer, fasting, and seeking God, you can receive everything you need. Don't be deceived by the enemy's tactics. Stand firm in your faith, trust in God's gifts, and walk in the authority He has given you.

# Reflective Questions:

1. Have you ever unknowingly engaged in spiritual practices that, in hindsight, may not have aligned with God's will? How did they impact your life and spiritual well-being?

2. What are some ways you can discern between worldly spiritual influences and the true guidance of the Holy Spirit?

3. If you have ever sought knowledge or power outside of God, how can you now surrender those experiences to Him and seek His truth instead?

# Interactive Activity:

Take a moment now to reflect on your own life. Have you ever felt spiritually blind? Perhaps there's something in your life you can't quite understand, or a force that feels like it's holding you back.

Take time to reflect on 1 Corinthians 12 and explore the different gifts of the Spirit. Take time to pray and ask God to open your spiritual eyes, as He did for me. Ask for His Holy Spirit to reveal any hidden things and Ask God to reveal to you your unique gifts, and pray for guidance on how to use them for His glory.

**Prayer:**

*Heavenly Father,*

*I thank You for the gift of life and for the care You have shown in creating me, granting me the opportunity to see another day. Lord, I ask that You help me to perceive the world as You do, with clarity and understanding. Reveal to me any areas in my life where I am blind, where I fail to see the unseen. Shine Your light upon these areas, Lord, so that I may gain wisdom, understanding, and spiritual growth through these experiences. I also ask for Your forgiveness for the times I have fallen short. As You open my spiritual eyes, align me more closely with Your will and help me to become more like You. In Jesus' name, I pray and give thanks.*

*Amen*

## Interactive Moment:

Reflect on how the enemy may try to influence your emotions or reactions. Do you recognize old patterns in your behavior or thoughts that lead you away from peace? Identify these areas in your life and invite God's healing to renew your mind by creating three healthy outlets you can use when these thoughts arise again. Examples: Listen to worship songs about peace, journal how you feel, go for a walk, or read a devotional on your feelings.

# Interactive Guide: Sharing Your Testimony

Consider your own past struggles. Maybe it's time for you to step out in faith and share your testimony or speak your truth.

1.  **Prayer for Open Doors.** Start by praying to God, asking Him to open doors that will allow you to be a willing vessel for His work. Pray for the courage and readiness to share your testimony with others in a way that will speak to their hearts and help them face the struggles they are currently going through.

2.  **Prepare to Share.** Be ready for the right opportunity to share your story. When God presents the chance, offer your testimony as a living example that struggles can be overcome through faith and perseverance. Your words might be the encouragement someone needs to keep going.

3.  **Seek Wisdom and Support.** If you feel burdened or weighed down, ask God to guide you toward a trusted spiritual advisor who can offer wisdom and insight. Having someone to walk alongside you can help you release the burdens you're carrying.

4.  **Journal Your Journey.** Keep a journal of your experiences as you go through this process. Writing down your thoughts, prayers, and reflections will

not only help you in your personal growth, but will also provide insight into how God is working in your life.

By following these steps, you'll not only find healing for yourself, but also become a source of strength for others. God's timing is perfect, and He will guide you to the right moments to be a light to those in need.

## Exercising Prophetic Gifts

One night, as the clock struck 11 p.m., I received an urgent call from a family member. Their voice trembled with fear, begging me to come immediately. There was an intensity in their words, an urgency I couldn't ignore. My heart raced as I rushed out the door, fear and dread mixing in the pit of my stomach. I had an inexplicable sense that something terrible was unfolding.

When I arrived, I stepped into a darkened room, the air thick with an unexplainable weight. A friend of theirs sat in the corner, hidden behind dark sunglasses. Something felt off, wrong, like the very room itself was alive with a heaviness that pressed against my chest. And then, a sharp pain shot through my heart, a pain I couldn't quite place until I realized it wasn't just physical. Something deeper was at play. It was spiritual.

As I approached him, despair hit me like a wave. His words were drenched in hopelessness, filled with a raw pain that pierced me deeply. He spoke of preferring death and the torment of hell to facing the unbearable weight of life. My heart broke for him, and I begged him to choose life, to turn to Christ, to find salvation and hope. But instead of the response I had hoped for, I was met with a dreadful smirk, a smile that sent a chill down my spine. The heaviness in the room thickened, and I knew in that moment this wasn't just a personal struggle. It was a battle far greater than anything I had ever imagined.

I left that room overwhelmed and emotionally drained, feeling as though I had been part of something far bigger than myself. I collapsed into my car and the tears came without warning, the weight of what I had witnessed crushing me. My hands shook as I called my mother and recounted the experience with a trembling voice. She listened carefully, and then gently warned me that as a new believer, I might not yet be ready to confront such darkness. She encouraged me to seek help from someone more seasoned in spiritual warfare.

With renewed urgency, I reached out to a dear friend. She came, armed with her Bible and anointing oil. Together, we set out to face the darkness. Neither of us had formal training, but we knew we had something greater on our side: the power of God. We prayed with every ounce of strength, anointing ourselves, the house, and crying out to God in the freezing rain. Every prayer seemed to intensify the oppressive atmosphere, but even through the fear, I began to feel God's strength rise within me.

A shift began to happen. In the midst of the brokenness, I saw a flicker of hope. I felt God's prompting to ask the person to remove their sunglasses. And when they did, what was hidden beneath the darkness was revealed—a wounded child, broken and lost, crying out for salvation. But there was still something darker, something insidious, clinging to them—an unyielding spirit of death that refused to let go. This battle was beyond my ability, beyond anything I could fight on my own. Only God could break those chains. I invited them to church, realizing this was no longer about me. It wasn't my will or desire that mattered, but God's power to heal, to deliver, and to save.

The next morning, drained and weary, I prayed for God's strength to continue this battle. As I entered the church, the atmosphere shifted. During praise and worship, I felt the Holy Spirit descend upon me like a warm embrace, filling me, surrounding me, lifting me higher than I had ever been. His presence was so tangible, so real, that I felt as though I was standing not on earth, but in the very presence of the Divine.

The friend from the night before had come to church. The Spirit of the Lord whispered to me, "Place your hand on their head, break the double mind, the doubt, the worry, the fear, the depression." I obeyed, and as my hand rested upon their head, I felt the heaviness begin to lift. God instructed me to speak directly to their heart, releasing the pain and weight. As I placed my hand upon their chest, they shed a tear—evidence of the Holy Spirit's work. I moved my hand to their stomach, sensing the deep-rooted despair, and prayed life into that broken place.

Then, under divine direction, I turned to the congregation, speaking with authority not of my own, but of God's. "This is a house of holiness," I declared. "God will not tolerate impurity here."

As I spoke, I felt the dark spirits in the room recoil, their anger rising. They tried to intimidate me, to shake my confidence, but in that moment, I remembered the promise: If God was with me, who could stand against me? The Holy Spirit filled me with strength, and as I called upon God's living water, the power of His Spirit surged through the room. People fell, others cried, some were set free from the bonds of darkness.

In the quiet of the altar call, I knelt, overwhelmed with gratitude. I heard the voice of the Spirit urging me to pray for the woman beside me. She was carrying a heavy burden, and the Holy Spirit guided me to speak life over her. As I prayed, I saw her rise from the weight of her pain, her steps more confident, more joyful. By the end of the service, she was walking, praising, her spirit renewed.

This experience changed me. I learned spiritual warfare isn't about our strength, but about yielding to God's power. It's in the surrender and trusting His authority that true healing and freedom happen. I learned that deliverance is not our victory to claim, but God's to carry out. And in that surrender, lives are transformed, chains are broken, and souls are set free.

# Prophetic Exercise:
# Engaging in Spiritual Warfare

1.  **Prayer of Surrender:** Begin by sitting in a quiet space, closing your eyes, and surrendering your will to God. Invite the Holy Spirit to guide you in the areas where spiritual warfare may be at work in your life or the lives of others. Ask for divine discernment to see beyond the surface and recognize the spiritual forces at play.

2.  **Stand in Authority:** Pray and declare your authority in Christ over any situation where you sense darkness or oppression. Acknowledge that spiritual warfare is not fought in your own strength, but in the power of God's might. Speak with confidence and authority, knowing that you are equipped with His Spirit.

3.  **Pray for the Broken:** Focus someone who is struggling with despair, hopelessness, or spiritual oppression. Ask God to reveal the hidden hurts and wounds beneath the surface. As you pray for them, imagine placing your hand on their head, chest, or

stomach as a symbol of God's healing power. Speak life and hope into their broken places, breaking any chains of darkness that may bind them.

4. **Declare Holiness:** In the spirit of authority, declare that God will not tolerate impurity or darkness in your life or in the lives of those you are praying for. Remind the enemy that the Spirit of the Lord has the final say and claim victory over every area where darkness tries to linger.

5. **Ask for the Holy Spirit's Strength:** Close by asking the Holy Spirit to infuse you with His strength, courage, and wisdom. Pray for His power to fill you as you step out in faith, knowing He's with you every step of the way. Trust in His divine power to transform lives and bring freedom where there is bondage.

## Prayer example:

*Heavenly Father,*

*I come before You today, surrendering my will and heart to Your divine guidance. Holy Spirit, lead me in this journey of spiritual warfare. Grant me the discernment to see beyond the surface and to recognize the hidden spiritual battles that are at work in my life and the lives of others. I stand firm in the authority given to me in Christ, knowing the battle is not mine, but Yours. In Your power, I declare victory over any darkness or oppression that seeks to linger in my life or in those I intercede for. I claim Your strength, Lord, and I speak life into every area of brokenness. As I pray for those who are hurting, I ask that Your healing power flows through me. Let my hands be instruments of Your de-*

*liverance, bringing hope, life, and freedom where despair and bondage exist. I break the chains of darkness with Your authority, and I declare that Your light will shine in the darkest places. I proclaim holiness over my life, my family, and all whom I pray for. I will not tolerate impurity or fear in my heart or in the hearts of those I intercede for. I remind the enemy that You, Lord, have the final word, and in You, there is victory. Holy Spirit, fill me with Your strength, courage, and wisdom as I step forward in faith. Empower me to move in Your might and trust in Your power to transform lives. May Your will be done, and may Your kingdom come.*

*In Jesus' name,*
*Amen.*

# Divine Dreams and Heavenly Visions

In this section, you are invited to walk with me through five powerful devotionals drawn from peaceful dreams, vivid visions, and real-life encounters with God. These aren't just diary entries—they are moments where the voice of Heaven broke through the noise of life, revealing God's heart, His guidance, and sometimes, His correction.

If you've ever questioned whether God still speaks, He does. Sometimes it's through a vision while you're fully awake, and other times it's in the stillness of sleep through dreams. And often, He'll use people, conversations, or even situations as divine messengers. Every devotional in this section was birthed from real encounters that God used to teach, guide, and awaken something in me. Now, I pray He does the same for you.

As you read, take your time. Don't rush the process. Invite the Holy Spirit to show you where these lessons apply to your own life. Some entries may affirm what you already know. Others may challenge you to surrender more deeply or step into what you've been avoiding. All are meant to draw you closer to God and prepare you to carry the spiritual keys He's placing in your hands.

Guided prayer before you begin:

*Father,*

*Open my heart, my mind, and my spirit to receive everything You want to show me during this devotional journey. Help me to recognize Your voice, discern Your direction, and understand the meaning behind each lesson. Remove distractions and stir my faith to believe that You still speak—and that You're speaking to me. I give You full access.*

*In Jesus' name,*

*Amen*

# Reflection Question:

Ask yourself: "Where in my life do I need to pause and ask, "God, what are You trying to show me?"

Write your thoughts or whisper them to God. He's listening—and ready to respond.

# Day 1: Keys to the Kingdom (Vision)

I saw myself cradled in the palm of Jesus' hand. His hand was so vast, I could kneel within it. I was broken and bare, pouring out tears with no words. There was no fear, only peace, only the sense that I was known and fully safe.

Then, the vision shifted. I saw Jesus walking through a city, His presence commanding, yet tender. He turned toward me with a gentle, firm voice and said, "It's time for you to walk, My child."

He set me down, and in His hand was a key. I took it with trembling hands. Before me appeared a tall, majestic gate—radiant and regal. As I placed the key in its lock and

turned it, the gate swung open to reveal a royal community—sacred ground prepared for me. My heart swelled
with awe and joy. I had been carried, comforted, and now,
called to walk into what He had ordained.

## Scripture: Revelation 3:8 (NIV)

"I know your deeds. See, I have placed before you an open
door that no one can shut. I know that you have little
strength, yet you have kept my word and not denied my
name."

## Devotional Reflection:

There's something sacred about being held by God. In our
lowest, most vulnerable moments, when our strength is
gone and our hearts are heavy, He doesn't push us forward—He holds us close. He lets us rest. But the time always
comes when He calls us to rise. Not in our own strength, but
in His authority.

The key He gives you is access—access to purpose, to
identity, to destiny. When you walk through the door, He
opens, you step into a reality no one else can claim. And
while your hands may still tremble, His hand never leaves
you. Too often we fear the next step, questioning if we're
ready. But God doesn't hand you the key unless He's already
secured the path.

This is your invitation to believe again—not in yourself, but in the One who carries you. The door is already
open. The gate is already unlocked. All that's left is for you
to walk.

## Wisdom Gem:

God is a man of His word—faithful and unchanging. He carries those who surrender, holding them in safety until
they're ready to walk. The key in your hand isn't given by

accident; it's proof that you are chosen, equipped, and invited into something greater. No man, no failure, not even fear can close the door God has opened. Walk through it.

**Prayer:**

> *Father,*
>
> *Thank You for holding me when I couldn't hold myself. Thank You for the peace that comes from knowing You see me, love me, and still choose me. Today, I accept the key You've placed in my hand. Give me courage to walk through the door You've opened. Let me never forget that my security isn't in the path— it's in the One who walks with me.*
>
> *In Jesus' name,*
> *Amen*

# Day 2: Harvest Hidden in the Hustle (Dream)

Have you ever felt like you were doing everything right, yet something still felt off—like one area of your life was glowing red while everything else appeared green?

In a dream, I found myself testing samples in a school-like setting outside my parents' home. All the test tubes lit up green—except one. That one turned red and flashed a 2.7. I stepped away briefly, but when I returned, everyone around me was crying. I didn't know what happened. No one would tell me. Then someone looked me in the eyes and asked, "Do you love your husband?"

Without hesitation, I said, "Yes, I love him very much."

But later, God revealed this wasn't just about earthly marriage. It was about my love for what He entrusted to

JAIRAE TAYLOR

me—the calling, the assignment, the work. He was asking, "Do you love what I gave you, even when it gets hard?"

A woman later stopped me at work and told me to read the story of Ruth, specifically, Ruth 2:7. When I read it, everything made sense. Ruth worked faithfully in a field that wasn't hers. She humbled herself, gleaned behind others, and labored under the sun, but it was her consistency that positioned her for divine favor.

## Scripture: Ruth 2:7 (NIV)

"Please let me glean and gather among the sheaves behind the harvesters."

## Scripture: Galatians 6:9 (NIV)

"Let us not become weary in doing good, for at the proper time we will reap a harvest if we do not give up."

## Devotional Reflection:

Life will test you. Some areas will flourish while others seem stuck on 2.7. It can be frustrating when you feel like you're doing all the right things and still see one area lag behind, but not every part of your life will harvest at the same time. That doesn't mean something is wrong—it means God is strategic.

The red test result may be revealing a part of your life that still needs healing, refinement, or patience. Don't ignore it, but don't let it discourage you, either. Ask the Lord what He's showing you. Sometimes, the very thing you want to walk away from is the exact thing tied to your breakthrough.

And what about the question, "Do you love your husband?" Maybe today, God is asking you, "Do you love what I've called you to? Will you stay faithful to the assignment when no one else sees it, celebrates it, or understands it?"

The tears in the dream represented the weight of your calling. Ministry, purpose, and legacy all cost something, and often, they come with hidden burdens. But like Ruth, you are not forgotten in the field. You are being watched, positioned, and prepared. When the time is right, the harvest will come not just in your hands, but in your heart.

**Wisdom Gem:**

Every kingdom promise has a process. The hustle is holy when it's rooted in obedience. The harvest is guaranteed, but it only comes to those who endure the season of planting, watering, and waiting.

**Prayer:**

*Lord,*

*Help me stay faithful in the work You've given me, even when it feels hard or unseen. Remind me that every seed I plant in obedience will produce fruit in Your timing. Strengthen me when I feel weary, and teach me to love the assignment—even in the hustle. I trust that the harvest is coming.*

*In Jesus' name,*
*Amen*

# Day 3: The Collapse of False Foundations (Dream)

I stood alone in the middle of the ocean, balanced precariously on a manmade circular platform. Around me, houses were being erected on something far too unstable to last.

Beneath me churned deep, unforgiving waters. A shark circled below like a silent threat. As I slipped toward the edge, panic rose in my chest. I struggled to hold on, not just from fear of the predator beneath, but because I finally understood the foundation itself was failing.

Soon after this dream, the Francis Scott Key Bridge in Baltimore collapsed. Watching it unfold, I realized this was more than coincidence; it was confirmation. The dream was a divine warning. We've built homes, systems, and even spiritual lives on platforms that aren't rooted in God. Like the houses on that floating circle, collapse is inevitable when the storm comes.

## Scripture: Matthew 7:26–27 (NLT)

"But anyone who hears my teaching and doesn't obey it is foolish, like a person who builds a house on sand. When the rains and floods come and the winds beat against that house, it will collapse with a mighty crash."

## Devotional Reflection:

This dream isn't just a personal warning. It's a national one. The platform was symbolic of manmade systems we trust: government, wealth, reputation, even spiritual platforms that look strong on the surface but are rooted in nothing but shifting waters. The shark wasn't just a threat; it represented what lurks beneath when we place our hope in appearances and not truth.

Like the Francis Scott Key Bridge, named after the man who penned the words to our national anthem, we are seeing symbolic landmarks fall. What once represented strength and liberty is crumbling. Why? Because we've put more trust in symbols than in the Savior.

This is a wake-up call to the Church, to the nation, and to every individual: check your foundation. What have you built your life upon? Are you building on God's Word—or on your own understanding, ambition, or fear? God is merciful enough to shake what is unsteady before it destroys us completely.

**Wisdom Gem:**

God doesn't bless what is built on pride, deception, or control. When Christ isn't your foundation, collapse isn't just possible, it's promised. Discern the ground you're standing on. If it's not rooted in truth, it can't hold you.

**Prayer:**

> *Father,*
>
> > *Reveal to me every place where I've built on unstable ground. Expose what looks strong but cannot hold. Give me the courage to leave behind every manmade platform that opposes Your will. I place my trust in You, the only true foundation. Help me to rebuild on the Rock.*
> >
> > *In Jesus' name,*
> > *Amen*

# Day 4: The Descent of Leadership and the Rise of the Watchers (Dream)

The dream began in what I thought was a hospital, but it was actually a health department. From the moment I stepped in, there was chaos. No clear signs. No guidance. I was supposed to find the "Healthy Families" office upstairs, but there was no direction. I entered the elevator with my family, hoping for clarity, but instead, we were trapped. The doors wouldn't close, and we had no idea where we were going.

Then he appeared. A man approached—someone who should have helped, but the moment our eyes met, I discerned his spirit: evil, corrupted, and dangerous. Without speaking, he struck the elevator, sending it plummeting downward. In that moment of terror, I grabbed a toddler no one else was holding and began to pray. My act of intercession became my anchor.

Later, I found myself in a boardroom filled with older professionals—seasoned leaders who had been in the system for decades. The phone rang. Accountability was calling. But when asked to provide answers, they panicked. No one knew what to say. They were unprepared. Disoriented. I sat in silence, the youngest in the room, watching it all unfold.

The final part of the dream brought me to a fragile bridge made of unstable material. I saw others walking across, but I sensed its danger and stepped off before it collapsed.

In the closing image, a dog dug through a box of clothes in a store. Garments were torn and tossed, symbolizing confusion around identity and covering. What was once sacred was being trampled.

## Scripture: Isaiah 3:12 (ESV)

"My people—infants are their oppressors, and women rule over them. O my people, your guides mislead you and they have swallowed up the course of your paths."

## Devotional Reflection:

This dream is a piercing diagnosis of our times. Systems once trusted—health, education, governance—are no longer safe by default. What was designed to give direction is now leading people into confusion and descent. The elevator, once a symbol of ease and upward mobility, became a trap. The man sent to help was a symbol of corruption in leadership, leading people not into life, but into spiritual descent.

The toddler represented innocence, the next generation, the vulnerable. While others panicked, I prayed, representing the call to intercede, to hold the ones others overlook, and to stay spiritually grounded when others descend into confusion.

In the boardroom, leaders were called to account with no answers. God is exposing the unprepared. Those who were trusted are being found wanting. And in their silence, a new voice is rising: the one who watches, discerns, and prays in the shadows.

Finally, the fragile bridge reminds us that not all popular paths are safe. Just because others walk it doesn't mean it's ordained. Discernment is your safety.

The final image—the dog digging through clothing—reveals the attack on identity in our culture. People's spiritual and emotional garments are being ripped apart by confusion, distraction, and lawlessness, but in the middle of this chaos, God is raising up the protectors and intercessors who are led by the Spirit of Truth.

## Wisdom Gem:

We're in a leadership crisis. Systems built to protect are disoriented, and those in power are unprepared, but God is raising up those with discernment, intercession, and the courage to step off collapsing paths.

The watchmen for God's people are now guarding their post and taking over territories.

**Prayer:**

> *Lord,*
>
> *Open my eyes to see what is truly happening beneath the surface. Give me the discernment to recognize false leadership, the courage to step off unstable paths, and the heart to intercede for those too vulnerable to stand alone. Help me be a voice of truth and hope in a world spiraling into deception. Raise me up as a watcher in this hour.*
>
> *In Jesus' name,*
> *Amen*

# Day 5: Strength Through Life Storms (Divine Encounter):

This wasn't a dream or vision. It was a real-life moment where God used multiple people to speak directly into my pain.

It started with a rough morning. I had three unexpected back-to-back financial setbacks. My husband and I scrambled, making phone calls and reaching out to agencies to find some kind of relief. Even after doing all we could, the weight still lingered. I felt drained, discouraged, and defeated.

Later that day, I felt an unusual urge to go to a store, something I don't normally do unless I need something specific. As I drove, I moved slowly, intentionally searching for the right place.

When I finally found the store and finished shopping, a woman parked beside me, waved me down, and said something I'll never forget: "I heard the Lord say pick your head up; it's not as bad as you think. Remember to adjust your crown, even if it tilts."

Her words stopped me in my tracks. Just a year prior, I had gifted my mother a bracelet that said, "Whenever you feel overwhelmed, remember who you are and straighten your crown."

It was as if God had reached through that stranger to remind me: "I see you. I know you. You're still Mine."

But that wasn't all. A coworker later messaged me with Matthew 11:28: "Come to me, all you who are weary and burdened, and I will give you rest."

She told me everything I needed was already in God. It was another gentle confirmation: He was with me.

A few days later, during worship at church, I broke. I cried out to God with everything in me, exhausted and empty. As I leaned forward over the chair, someone came behind me, embraced me, and whispered that very same verse—Matthew 11:28—in my ear. It was clear: God had something to say. And He was going to make sure I heard Him.

## Scripture: Matthew 11:28 (NIV):

"Come to me, all you who are weary and burdened, and I will give you rest."

## Scripture: Luke 12:32 (NLT):

"So don't be afraid, little flock. For it gives your Father great happiness to give you the Kingdom."

## Devotional Reflection:

Sometimes, life hits without warning. Financial hardship. Mental weariness. Emotional pressure. It all adds up. And when it does, it can feel like you're barely holding it together.

But God isn't silent in your struggle. He sends confirmation when you're least expecting it, whether through a stranger in a parking lot, a text from a coworker, or a scripture spoken in the middle of worship. These aren't coincidences; they're divine appointments.

The message God gave me—adjust your crown—wasn't just poetic; it was prophetic. It was His way of saying, "Lift your head, daughter. You still belong to Me. Your identity is not in your crisis. It's in your connection to the Kingdom."

When you're in the storm, it's easy to believe you've been forgotten. But rest assured God sees you. He hears your cries, and He responds. Sometimes not in grand gestures, but in soft, sacred moments where His love becomes undeniably real.

This is your reminder: Don't worry. Don't quit. And don't forget who you are.

## Wisdom Gem:

When life feels heavy, God doesn't leave you to carry it alone. He sends reminders through people, through scripture, and whispers in quiet places. Don't overlook divine messages wrapped in ordinary moments. His comfort is always closer than it seems.

## Prayer:

*Father,*

*Thank You for showing up in the middle of my chaos. Thank You for sending words of comfort through others when I couldn't find strength on my own. I give You my burdens. I lay down my worries. Help me to lift my head again, to adjust my crown, and to remember that I am Yours, even when the storm rages around me. Teach me to rest in Your presence.*

*In Jesus' name,*

*Amen*

# A Call to the Nation

The first time God spoke to me about the state of the nation, I was overwhelmed with fear. Out of all the people in the world, why did He choose me? I was an introvert, terrified of public speaking, and unsure of how I could possibly reach an entire nation with His message.

Yet, God often calls the least likely to speak His truth, and I found myself grappling with this overwhelming responsibility. I was unworthy, lacking confidence, and deeply aware of my own limitations, but God has a way of calling His people to fulfill His purpose, even when it seems impossible. For years, I wrestled with this call, feeling incapable and inadequate. But through every moment of doubt and fear, I could hear the groanings of the Spirit urging me to fulfill the task.

One night, God sent me a vivid dream that shook me to my core and revealed His heart for the nations. It was 3 a.m. when I woke up from the dream. I had seen a fire in a parking lot north of where I lived. People stood by watching it burn, but no one was doing anything to stop it. The fire grew bigger, and as I approached it, I noticed others joining me. We formed a circle, holding hands as the fire grew fiercer. And then, from the heavens, a light descended, and the fire was extinguished.

Confused and alarmed, I lay in bed, trying to understand the meaning of the dream. And then, I heard a clear, stern voice speak to me: "Pray for the nation, for it is on fire and burning with wickedness. Take My light, gather those willing to listen, and unite as one to follow Me. Those who obey My Word will overcome the fire. Those who ignore My call will face My wrath. Do not fear, for I am with you. Take this Word to My people, for I hear their cries. I am alive. Do not be dismayed. Remember the many times I have saved you. Be strong and courageous."

I searched the Scriptures and found confirmation in Psalm 34:7–8: "The angel of the Lord encamps around those who fear Him, and He delivers them." Further verses in Psalms echoed this message of rescue and judgment. The dream was a warning: the nation was burning in its own wickedness, and unless people turned back to God, they would face His wrath. Yet for those who listened, there was hope and restoration.

God has a pattern of calling nations to repentance. He has spoken to His people throughout history, warning them of impending judgment, but always offering deliverance for those who turn back to Him. This was His message in the dream: to sound the alarm, to unite His people, and to call them to stand firm in His Word.

Months later, another dream came—a dream of a volcanic eruption. I had only an hour to prepare and warn my loved ones. I saw the smoke rising from the volcano, and fear gripped me. I had been warned before, but I had procrastinated, thinking I had time. As the eruption drew nearer, I urged my family to gather their belongings and seek safety.

The Holy Spirit reminded me of an ark under the volcano that would shelter all who were willing to seek refuge there. In the Old Testament, the Ark of the Covenant symbolized God's presence and protection. This ark under the volcano represented God's refuge for His people in the midst of disaster. Yet, despite my warnings, many ignored them, distracted by irrelevant concerns. Some hesitated, while others outright rejected the call. Only a few were ready when the eruption came.

As we made our way to safety, I could hear the cries of those left behind, but it was too late. The time for preparation had passed. I was reminded of 1 John 2:18: "Dear children, this is the last hour; and as you have heard that the antichrist is coming, even now many antichrists have come. This is how we know it is the last hour."

The volcano was a symbol of God's call to salvation just before His wrath descends. The people left behind represent those distracted by the world's temporary things, who will realize too late that they should have repented and turned to God. God's message is clear: Prepare your hearts now, for the time is short. The world is on the brink of disaster, and many are oblivious to the coming judgment. But those who listen to God's call and seek refuge in Him will be saved. The volcano, like the smoke from Mount Sinai in Exodus 19:18–19, symbolizes God's holiness and the trembling fear that comes when His wrath is near. We must go toward the fire, not away from it, trusting in His protection, even in the most terrifying circumstances. God's mercy has been delayed, but it won't last forever.

In another dream, I heard God's voice: "I have delayed My wrath on the people, calling them to turn back to Me. But if they do not listen, I will come, and they will see that I am the Lord."

His patience has been long, but He will not wait forever. The time is now to turn from wickedness and seek His face.

As I continued to wrestle with these vivid dreams, God sent another warning through my dreams. In the dream I was riding in a van with my family when armed men surrounded us. We sought refuge in an abandoned police station, but the attackers relentlessly pursued us. I tried to defend my family, but my gun jammed every time I tried to fire. I did my best to protect everyone in the car. Moments after my gun jammed, a bomb was thrown at the vehicle, causing a family member to burn, but I threw a blanket on her and immediately extinguished the fire.

It was a powerful dream. The sword of the Spirit, the Word of God, is ready for us to use, but too often, we fail to act. We have the tools for spiritual warfare, yet we let fear and hesitation prevent us from using them.

The bombs in the dream represented the increasing attacks from evil, while the family member who caught fire symbolized the need for faith to protect and cover those we love. As the attacks came, I found the strength to cover her with a blanket, demonstrating the power of faith to extinguish the flames of destruction.

In one of my final dreams concerning the nation, God showed me The Child, the Bridge, and the Reckoning. In the dream, I found myself inside a massive truck—maybe a bus—traveling across a long, narrow bridge suspended over deep, restless waters.

What caught my attention immediately was who was driving. A little girl, no more than ten years old, sat behind the wheel. Her feet barely reached the pedals. Her father was beside her, clearly the one guiding the journey, yet he had allowed her to shift the gears. She looked nonchalant, carefree, even reckless. It was as if she didn't grasp the weight of the responsibility she'd been given.

I locked eyes with her and gave her a firm, pleading look that said, *sit down, focus, and take this seriously*. She seemed to understand and adjusted her posture, sitting more attentively, hands on the wheel. But even as she straightened up, the atmosphere shifted.

The winds picked up, and the ocean below us began to roar. Waves rose violently against the bridge as if they were trying to pull us under. The rain began to fall in sheets. The bridge turned frighteningly narrow, and suddenly, the tires beneath us lost traction and we started to hydroplane. For a moment, it felt like we were spinning out of control. I held my breath, bracing for the worst. And then—miraculously—we regained balance.

But just as relief began to set in, the bridge came to a dead end. There was nowhere left to go. And in slow, surreal motion, we plunged from the edge into the raging sea below. Time seemed to slow. Fear tightened my chest. As the bus fell, my thoughts weren't just on survival—they were on eternity. I began to cry out to God, repenting with everything in me, not just for myself, but for Josh. I turned to him in desperation and said, "Do you want to try and get out? Climb through the window? Or are we just going to stay here and die like this?"

He looked at me with a calm resolve and replied, "Let's just stay. It'll be easier than facing what's out there."

Those words broke something in me. Easier? Maybe. But easier didn't mean right. I couldn't let us give up. I kept praying and calling on God, and just like that, the scenery shifted. We weren't in the water anymore.

The bus landed in front of a building that looked like a school or a center of some kind. We stepped off and went inside, where we were welcomed by three authority figures. One was an Asian woman, another a Black man, and possibly a white man. People began to gather. I was told I wasn't originally on the list—but I had been added.

The room erupted in applause. I took a seat, humbled and curious, and pulled out my notepad, ready to take notes. On the board at the front of the room, I saw the word ISIS, along with a few others I couldn't quite remember. The leaders were preparing to teach us—not just general lessons, but the reason behind the crash, the journey, the storm, and the fall. I leaned over to the person next to me and whispered, "I've seen this before. I've had dreams like this since I was a child."

He looked at me with understanding in his eyes and said, "Me too. That's why we're here."

This dream wasn't just a warning; it was a message wrapped in symbols, showing the condition of a generation, the role of spiritual leadership, and the choices we're all faced with in times of crisis.

The child behind the wheel represented immaturity taking the lead—youthfulness being handed authority too early with little understanding of the danger ahead. The father's passive role revealed the condition of many leaders today—present, but allowing the vulnerable to steer with no firm direction.

The bridge symbolized the path many of us are on right now: high above the chaos, but growing narrower by the moment. The storm was what we feel in our spirits—the warning of coming judgment, the instability of our surroundings, and the battle between control and surrender.

When the bus began to hydroplane, it reflected what happens when we move too fast without being grounded in God. And when the bridge gave out, it revealed what many are feeling: we've run out of road. What's ahead isn't predictable anymore—it's a fall into the unknown.

The plunge into the ocean represented a moment of reckoning. That terrifying place between life and death, between surrender and panic. My cry to God was an act of spiritual awakening. But Josh's response—choosing the "easier" death rather than fighting for survival—exposed something deeper. It showed how many have grown tired. Tired of trying. Tired of hoping. Ready to give up rather than wrestle with what's beyond the window. And yet, when we prayed, heaven responded.

The building represented a place of divine instruction, a place for the chosen, the set apart, and those who had survived their fall. I wasn't originally on the list, but grace added my name. That moment reminded me God doesn't count people out the way we do. There's always room at His table for the repentant and hungry.

The word ISIS on the board felt symbolic—not just of terror in the natural, but spiritual deception, destruction, and strongholds God is preparing His people to confront and overcome.

The leaders were sent to prepare and train us. The dreams we've had, the visions we've seen, the storms we've endured all led here. We aren't alone; there are others who've seen what we've seen. And now, God is gathering us for instruction, revelation, and deployment.

God showed me the overall message of the alarming dreams I was having. The message was that we must not be silent. The responsibility to warn others of the coming judgment is on us. As Ezekiel 33:11–13 reminds us, if we fail to speak out, the blood of the lost will be on our hands, but if we faithfully deliver God's message, those who listen will be saved, and we will be spared from the consequences of their sin.

Now at the end of this journey—after dreams, visions, divine encounters, and sacred warnings—I will release the audible voice of God. His words thundered in my spirit. They weren't soft or symbolic. They were a declaration from the throne of Heaven. He said, "For I, the Lord, have come to My people as a warning of what's to come. I, the Lord, who is mighty and strong, come before the people to bring judgment upon the earth. You people who are wicked and low, I see and I know all of your ways. I see and I know your hearts. You cannot hide from Me—because you have already been found.

"I will destroy the land just as I destroyed Jerusalem and Judah. You think you can escape because My wrath has not been shown in a long time. But understand—I've been watching you for years upon years, and still, you have not returned to Me.

"I brought you out of captivity. I delivered your ancestors with My own hand. And still, you go astray. You disregard Me as if I did nothing for you. But to those who seek eternal life, seek Me now while I can still be found. For there will come a day when I will be silent. Though you cry out, I will turn away—eyes that do not see, ears that do not hear.

"I sent messengers to you. I sent voices with warnings. I sent dreams. I gave you signs. And yet you ignored them. You mocked them. You delayed your repentance.

"I love you, but why have you mistreated Me? Why have you not loved Me the way I have loved you? Why do you chase godless things and bow to idols? Why do you defile My name in false worship? You won't sit at My feet. You won't seek My face. All I ever asked for was your presence.

"You are My children. I adopted you into sonship when you believed in My Son. But how you have forsaken Me— as though I committed adultery against you. Yet, it is you who have been unfaithful. Still, I take you back. I always take you back when you cry. But then you return to your evil ways. Again and again.

"This is My warning: return to Me with a sincere heart. Love Me. For I am a compassionate God—slow to anger, rich in mercy. Honor the covenant I made with you. Remember it. For I, the Lord, will honor it if you obey Me. Obey what I have spoken—now and in the past.

"Because the day is coming when I will no longer hold back My anger. I will destroy every being, every creature, every town, every city. I will release mass destruction, and

I will not stop until My anger is satisfied and the earth is purified.

"For I, the Lord, have spoken. Now you must choose the path you will walk. Choose wisely."

We are in the last days, and God is raising up watchmen to sound the alarm. The time to act is now. The nation is on fire. The volcanic eruption is imminent. But even now, God offers an ark of salvation to all who will listen. The question is: Will you answer His call?

Don't wait for the storm to overtake you. The time to prepare is now.

Turn from wickedness.

Seek the Lord.

Follow Him with all your heart.

God is calling His people to take a stand, to unite in faith, and to sound the trumpet for all to hear. This is a warning—a plea for the nations to return to their Creator before it's too late.

As you reach the end of this book, I want to offer a word of encouragement and clarity: If, back in Chapter 4, you hesitated or chose not to accept Christ's invitation to walk with you, but now feel your heart being stirred, I invite you to go back and re-read that chapter. Speak the prayer. Invite Him in. He's waiting with open arms.

To those who already said "yes" and accepted Christ as Lord, stay strong. The journey may not be easy, but you are never walking it alone. Lean into His strength. Trust in His timing and let His peace anchor you when the winds rise.

To everyone who has completed this book, I pray that it has enriched your spirit and provided you with the discernment and clarity needed for the days ahead. Let these pages be more than stories. Let them become strategy. Let them become your preparation, your posture, and your prayer.

The Kingdom is calling. The keys are in your hand. And God's light will never leave your path.

Keep pressing forward. The best is yet to come.

# About the Author

Jairae Taylor is an accomplished author, poet, gospel artist, and songwriter whose life's mission is to reach the broken, the overlooked, and the voiceless. Born and raised in a small town on the west side of Salisbury, Maryland, Jairae grew up in a tough neighborhood where survival often took precedence over dreams. Though she was always shy and timid, she stood out for her intelligence and determination, earning  honor roll recognition and being selected for a competitive STEM program while still in middle school. Even in an environment marked by struggle, her brilliance quietly shone.

As the middle child of four sisters in a household with both parents, Jairae often found herself in solitude, watching, reflecting, and learning to process life in silence. At just thirteen years old, she began to rap and write as a form of survival—an outlet to express the feelings she buried deep within, the kind of emotions she couldn't find the words to say out loud. What began as a private release quickly revealed itself to be a divine gift. Her lyrics and journal entries became a place where the silent cries of a lost teenage girl could finally be heard.

Her ministry calling is deeply rooted in Psalm 82:4: "Rescue the weak and the needy; deliver them from the hand of the wicked." This scripture became the foundation for Oasis Evolve, the nonprofit organization she founded to restore women and families battling adversities she once faced: domestic violence, identity loss, and spiritual trauma. Through Oasis Evolve, Jairae lives out her divine assignment to rescue, to restore, and to rebuild lives through truth, compassion, and action.

A prophetic voice and seer, Jairae receives dreams and visions from God, which she uses to guide others into spiritual alignment and personal transformation. Her deep connection to nature serves as a sacred place of rest, renewal, and divine communion, where her spirit is strengthened, and her purpose is refined.

In addition to her creative and spiritual callings, Jairae is a passionate community advocate, a loving wife, and a faithful daughter of the Most High God. Her life is a living testament to the redemptive power of Christ. Through every word she writes and every soul she encounters, Jairae seeks to lead others from the shadows of pain into the light of restoration and purpose.